BEGINNING POLO

T5-AFR-601

The author on his Arab gelding "Montez"

BEGINNING POLO

Harry Disston

SOUTH BRUNSWICK AND NEW YORK:
A. S. BARNES AND COMPANY
LONDON: THOMAS YOSELOFF LTD

© 1973 by A. S. Barnes and Co., Inc.

A. S. Barnes and Co., Inc.
Cranbury, New Jersey 08512

Thomas Yoseloff Ltd
108 New Bond Street
London W1Y OQX, England

Library of Congress Cataloging in Publication Data
Disston, Harry, 1899–
    Beginning polo.

    1. Polo. I. Title.
GV1011.D57   796.35′3   72–5186
ISBN 0-498-01214-X

PRINTED IN THE UNITED STATES OF AMERICA

OTHER BOOKS BY HARRY DISSTON

Equestionnaire
Horse and Rider
Know about Horses
Riding Rhymes
Handbook for the Novice Horseman
Elementary Dressage
Dressage Writers and Readers
Quiz Questions for the U.S. Pony Clubs

GV
1011
.D57

Dedicated
to
my very good friend
the late
PAUL BROWN
who depicted polo with so much
skill and understanding, contributed
immensely to popularizing the game,
and helped me immeasurably by
illustrating my early writing.

34370

CONTENTS

PREFACE

Polo, following a marked decline from 1930 to 1960, is again trending upward in player and spectator participation.

In 1930, at the height of the game's popularity, the United States Polo Association's handicap list included some 3,000 players, about 1,200 of them serving in the Regular Army. In 1940 the list included only some 1,200 players and by 1960 the number had dropped to less than 700. But by 1971, the handicap list had increased to about 1,100 players.

In recent years, a considerable interest in polo has developed among teenagers through the United States Pony Clubs and the 4–H horse project groups throughout our country. Adults as well are starting their polo careers in the simpler and much less expensive area of paddock and arena polo.

Over the past sixty years, many books have been written about polo. Almost all of them approach the subject from the viewpoint of one who has a reasonable knowledge of— and some experience with—the game. This book attempts to present the game—what it takes to play it and how to learn to play it—from the viewpoint of the beginner. Much thought was given to the organization and presentation of the subject matter so that it might be of the greatest help and encouragement to the beginner.

In all games and sports, one learns by personal instruction and experience; a book can only be a guide. I trust that this is a good one.

ACKNOWLEDGMENTS

With great appreciation, enthusiasm, and respect I acknowledge the assistance of those who helped with the preparation of this book: Rodger Rinehart; Dr. E. D. Vere Nicoll; Paul Summers; Edgar Staples; Colonel C. Hancock Reed; Franklin Wawner; Garrett Kirksey and Adalbert von Gontard, who reviewed and commented on the typescript; John J. ("Jake") Carle, who, in addition to commenting on the text, took and provided from his files a large number of still and action photographs, many of which are among the illustrations in this book; Tom Lavery; Zenas Colt; George Haas; Colonel James Spurrier; Hal Vita; the Meadowbrook Club on Long Island and the United States Polo Association, who provided important photographs and diagrams and permission to use them. My thanks also to the Miller Harness Company of New York, who gave permission to reprint the examples of polo tack.

I must, with pleasant nostalgia, acknowledge also the basic contribution to what I have written by my teammates on the Fort Neck, Stanwich, Brush Farms, Seventh Regiment, Eighth Cavalry, and Squadron A teams, and our opponents on the playing field. And I acknowledge the contribution to my polo education made by the teams I have observed as an umpire, referee, reporter, and spectator, and by the fun games and scrimmages at Farmington, Keswick, and Hidden Hill in Virginia.

To Gloria Rennolds and Dudley Gaines, who typed the

manuscript and called to my attention words they did not understand, I am grateful.

And I acknowledge happily the considerable help my wife, Katie, provided by way of editorial comment and patience.

BEGINNING POLO

1
THE GAME

Polo is a game played by two teams of four mounted horsemen; the object is to hit a small wooden ball with a wooden mallet through goal posts at the end of a turf (or, infrequently, dirt) field. It is properly called "The Galloping Game."

The playing field is 300 yards long and 160 yards wide, and is bounded on each side by wooden sideboards ten inches high and an inch thick. The goal posts are set eight yards apart at the center of each end of the field; they are ten feet high and light enough to break if collided with.

The mallet carried by each player has a cane shaft and a wooden head, is about fifty inches long and weighs a little over a pound. The polo ball—usually made of willow root and sometimes of bamboo root, and covered with a glassy white enamel—is about three-and-one-quarter inches in diameter and weighs about four-and-one-half ounces. This is slightly larger and a little lighter than a baseball.

The four players on a side are identified—usually by numbers on the front and back of their shirts—as Number 1, Number 2, Number 3, and Back (Number 4). Numbers 1 and 2 are offensive players; Number 3 is the pivot (both offensive and defensive); the Back is defensive. Players are required to wear protective caps or helmets.

The game is divided into six periods (commonly called *chukkers*) of seven-and-one-half minutes each with a 4-minute interval between them. Ends are changed after each goal and the sounding of a horn signifies that seven minutes have elapsed, although the play may go on for another thirty seconds.

A team scores a goal when one of its players hits the ball through the opposing team's posts. Each goal scored counts one.

The polo mount is not a pony. It is a horse—a small horse, to be sure—but not a pony. The popular term *pony* goes back some sixty years to the days when there was a height limit and polo mounts were indeed ponies.

Fouls—generally incidents and situations which are dangerous or impede the speed of play—are penalized by a variety of "free" hits at goal by the side fouled. The free hits vary in terms of distance from the goal, placement of the ball, and as to whether or not the defending opponents are permitted to attempt to block the free hit. The variety of free hit is determined by the severity of the foul. A mounted umpire—or two—remains on the field to bowl in the ball which starts play, to stop play when fouls are committed, and to assess penalties.

Individual handicaps, assigned by the United States Polo Association, provide team totals which are used to attempt to equalize differences in experience and ability of opposing teams. Individual handicaps range from zero (about fifty percent of the players are so rated) to ten (which handicap has never been carried by more than four players at one time and seldom by more than one). In recent years, only three percent of the players have been at five or over. The team with the lower total handicap starts the game credited with a number of goals equal to the difference between its total handicap and the total handicap of the other team.

The three basic essentials of success in polo are: 1) a mount that is fast, handy, easily controlled, and not unduly excited; 2) reliable and accurate stroking (hitting); 3) effective team play.

Regulation, outdoor, polo may be played with certain modifications. *Paddock polo* is played outdoors without kneeboards and on a small turf field. *Arena polo* is played outdoors or indoors, in an area about a third the size of a regulation field, with kneeboards. These are about four feet high and entirely enclose the playing area; a team scores in Arena Polo by hitting a backboard rather than hitting *through* goal posts. The fields of these modified games are generally one hundred yards long or less and from twenty-

High goal polo

five to forty yards wide. In both Paddock and Arena Polo, there are only three players on a side (Number 1, Number 2, and Back); an inflated leather ball—in appearance like a diminutive basketball—is used instead of the wooden ball. The leather ball is larger than the wooden ball—about four-and-one-half inches in diameter—and weighs about six ounces. The mallets are the same as those used in outdoor regulation polo.

Polo at Keswick, Virginia (near Charlottesville)

Arena polo outdoors at Farmington Hunt Club, Virginia

Indoor polo at Shallow Brook, Connecticut

2
HISTORY

Polo is an ancient game. It was played by the Persians about 600 B.C. not too differently from the way it is played today. It may have been played earlier, but we have no records to indicate this. From Persia the game was introduced to India and Tibet, to China and Japan. The Chinese and Japanese modified the game considerably, using a small hole in the goal area as a target; the game thus became a kind of mounted lacrosse. Over the centuries there was, however, little change in the way the game was played in Persia, India, and Tibet. The number of players on a side varied from eight to as many as the playing field could accommodate. Emphasis was on individual possession of the ball, so that there must have been much clever and skillful dribbling, and on individual scoring.

The word *polo* comes from the Tibetan *pulu,* meaning ball. In Persia, the game was known as *changan,* meaning mallet.

Polo was introduced to England, and thence to Europe and America, from India, where the game was imported from Persia, it seems, sometime in the sixteenth century. In the 1850s we find the game flourishing in the Indian provinces of Bengal, Calcutta, Manipur, and Punjab. And we know that some Europeans and some British Army officers were playing polo then with Indians on Indian ponies in Calcutta.

Polo was introduced to England, it is said, by the Tenth Hussars as a result of their reading in the English sporting magazine *The Field* about the game as played in India. This was in 1869. The game was played on Hounslow Heath, near London, with crudely improvised mallets and balls and on small Irish ponies standing only 12 or 13 hands. There were eight on a side, no rules, and only two long periods. The pace of the game was a slow canter or trot. Other British Cavalry regiments soon took up the game and several inter-regimental matches were played.

Polo was formalized in the West by London's socially prominent Hurlingham Club in 1872. General and specific rules were established, among them a rule designating the number of players on a side. The number was first set at five, but soon changed to four. The game became popular and spectator attendance was large.

James Gordon Bennett is credited with introducing polo to the United States in 1876 on his return from a visit to England, where he had seen a game played at the Hurlingham Club. He brought with him a supply of mallets and balls, procured a number of ponies from Texas, and began playing polo with his friends in the indoor arena at Dickels Riding Academy in New York City. In the spring, the players transferred their activity to the Jerome Park racetrack infield in Westchester County, New York. Soon the Westchester Polo Club was organized by Bennett and his friends.

The fashionable Meadow Brook Club, near Westbury, Long Island, took up the game in 1879; then the Queens County and Brighton Polo Clubs—both on Long Island—and the Buffalo Polo Club were organized. Match games between these clubs attracted large crowds. It is recorded that about 10,000 spectators witnessed an 1879 match between teams representing the Westchester and Queens County Clubs.

Handicapping of individual players and teams—a great step forward for the new and growing game—was introduced in 1888.

Polo at the Meadow Brook Club, Long Island, near the turn of the century. Note the absence of protective headgear.

In 1890, the United States Polo Association was organized. It published rules of play, listed and handicapped players, and sponsored and conducted a number of national and regional tournaments. Until its organization, the Hurlingham Club rules governed club, match, and tournament play in the United States.

Polo players and ponies at the turn of the century at the Meadow Brook Club. Notice the docked tails, absence of draw reins, and the typical "hunting seat" of the time.

Just before the turn of this century, the United States Cavalry regiments took up polo—an ideal sport for developing several of the characteristics desired in cavalry commanders. Cavalry officers quickly became enthusiastically active in encouraging the game on all of the Army's widespread posts and stations. Polo was soon played at West Point and included in the cadets' instruction in horsemanship. Before long, officers of all branches of the Army (in those days most were mounted) became interested in polo, and soon the Army Polo Association was formed; in 1902 it merged with the United States Polo Association.

The British Hurlingham team which opposed the United States in the first international polo match, played for the Westchester Cup at Newport, Rhode Island in 1886

The United States international team which opposed England in 1909, 1911, and 1913

In two international matches, United States Army polo teams met British Army teams—at Meadow Brook on Long Island in 1923 and near London in 1925. The United States Army teams won both matches.

The first international match (between the United States and England) was played at Newport, Rhode Island, in 1886 for the Westchester Cup. The British won. A Rockaway Hunting Club team (from Long Island) travelled to England in 1902 in an attempt to regain the Cup. Although they lost the match two games to one on the Hurlingham Club grounds, that match had a long-lasting favorable result. The Americans were impressed with the importance of team play

The polo field at Meadow Brook

and also with the advantage of a greater variety of strokes. In 1909 the United States team went to England and brought back the coveted Cup. Two years later a British team came to Long Island to retrieve it but lost two matches by a narrow margin. They did, however, regain the Cup in 1914. The international matches for the historic Westchester Cup were suspended during World War I.

In 1921, the United States team traveled to the Hurlingham Club and won two games handily to retrieve the Cup. The British sent teams to the Meadow Brook Club in 1924, 1927, 1930 and 1939, and the United States sent a team to Hurlingham in 1936; the United States won all of these matches. The Cup has not been in competition since 1939.

International matches were also instituted between the United States and Argentina and Mexico. The Americas Cup was contested with Argentina six times from 1928 at the Meadow Brook Club on Long Island to 1969 in Buenos

The United States against Argentina in Buenos Aires, 1966

Aires—twice in the United States and four times in Argentina. The United States won two of the six matches, and also three matches for the General Manuel Avilla Camacho Cup, one in 1941 and two in 1946. These were played one each in Mexico City, at the Meadow Brook Club on Long Island, and at San Antonio, Texas.

Until 1921, penalties for fouls were imposed by the deduction of a quarter, half, or whole goal from the fouling side's score. At that time, the present penalties, comprising a variety of free hits, were introduced.

Until 1899, the height limit for polo mounts had been 13.3 hands (in the earliest days, 12.2 hands). In 1916 the height limit, which for a long time had been 14.2 hands (a pony), was abolished. Soon it became the general practice to play small thoroughbreds or part thoroughbreds standing 15.0 to 15.3 hands.

During the latter 1920s and the 1930s "countryside polo" grew steadily in popularity. This is polo played with only two mounts (sometimes only one) on smaller, uneven, ungroomed fields, for groups of friends, relatives, and sympathizers. In the West, cowhands took up the game in earnest, generally playing on oiled, "skinned" (grassless) fields. Any college which had a mounted R.O.T.C. unit fielded a polo

Typical polo ponies at the turn of the century. Note the simplicity of bits, the absence of caveson nosebands, and the docked tails.

team. The mounts were limited in their ability, but so were those of the opponents. Such limited polo required hard work, dedication and initiative, but not wealth.

Along with the growth of "countryside" polo, and then replacing it, grew what is now called "arena polo" (played indoors and outdoors). This kind of polo became an increasing attraction for players and spectators alike. It was featured at every National Guard mounted organization's armory and at every riding club that had an indoor ring.

Following a decrease in polo activity just after World War II, there has been a slow but positive resurgence of the game, on regulation fields, in arenas, and on short fields. In the last two decades the center of activity of polo has moved to the Middle West, away from previous centers in California and, of course, the East, where the Meadow Brook Club (which had seven regulation playing fields) had long exercised a colorful and positive domination over the game. Appropriately, Chicago, close to the center of the United States, is now recognized as polo's capital.

While it is most unlikely that polo in our country will ever reach the level of popular appeal it has in Argentina, as the game approaches a sort of modern centenary, a continued healthy long life and bright future in the United States appears a reasonable prospect.

3
THE BALL

The standard polo ball is made of willow or bamboo root. It is varnished white, is about three and one-quarter inches in diameter and weighs about four ounces. Thus it is a little larger and lighter than a baseball. The regulation wooden balls cost about $9.00 a dozen. In 1970 a plastic ball was developed and used to a limited extent. This ball lasts longer and costs about the same as the wooden ball.

A ball becomes unusable because it receives numerous dents from the players' mallets and because particles are chipped off it. Therefore, about two balls are used per period—a dozen during the average game.

"Old" balls which are not too severely damaged, may be used, to a limited extent, to practice stroking. If, however, your practice involves following the ball with several strokes or passing, you should use a new ball which rolls true and fast on the turf.

The ball used for paddock, arena and indoor polo is very different. Since it must be adaptable to irregular footing, to bouncing off knee boards (arena and indoors), and to a much smaller playing surface than that of the standard field, it is made of leather inflated by a rubber bladder. The "indoor" (or arena) ball looks like a miniature soccer ball or

"Outdoor" (regular) polo balls of bamboo (left) and willow root (right)

Indoor or arena (inflated leather) ball compared with a regular wooden (bamboo) "outdoor" ball

basketball. It is white, about four-and-one-half inches in diameter and weighs about six ounces.

When hit with an equivalent force, the "indoor" ball does not travel as far as the regulation wooden ball; nor has it as much roll.

An "indoor" ball will last for a long time—a year or two. Even if a horse should step squarely on it, a new bladder will usually put it in shape again. If the ball loosens or bursts at the seams, a shoe repairman or saddler can quickly repair it. The bladder and valve must be replaced from time to time and the ball periodically cleaned and white-washed. It must, of course, be kept inflated to its maximum pressure—about 18 pounds. "Indoor" balls cost about $15.00 each. An individual would want to have one or perhaps two; a club, a half dozen—all in good condition.

In order to preserve the expensive "indoor" balls for scrim-mage and match play, many individuals and clubs practice with inexpensive toy rubber balls purchased in variety or department stores. They are frequently multi colored or of a shiny solid color; this does not matter as long as the ball is not a solid green or brown, which is difficult to see on the field. (In any event, if you do not like the color, you can paint the ball white.) Balls close in size to an "indoor" ball may be bought for from 35 to 75 cents.

4
THE MALLET

The average polo mallet weighs about a pound and is fifty inches long from the ground side of the head to the top of the grip. It consists of: 1) the head, 2) the shaft and 3) the grip. A fabric thong is attached to the grip.

The head is shaped like a cigar tapered slightly at each end. The shaft is inserted into the head at an angle of about 80° and the ball is hit by the long side of the head (not, as in croquet, the end) at or near where the shaft is inserted.

Some mallets are lighter or heavier than others: weight varies according to the weight of the head, the type and length of cane used for the shaft, and the type of wrapping of the grip. Weight differences are, however, within a range of only two to three ounces.

The length of the mallet is a matter of individual choice affected by 1) the height of your mount at the saddle and the width of its barrel, 2) the length of your stroking arm, and 3) the manner in which you usually hit the ball—i.e. whether you reach down for it or sit comparatively upright. Therefore you may need mallets of different lengths for each of your different mounts—and at least two of each length (in the event that one breaks). To start and to experiment with, you will probably want a 50-inch and a 51-inch mallet

THE POLO MALLET

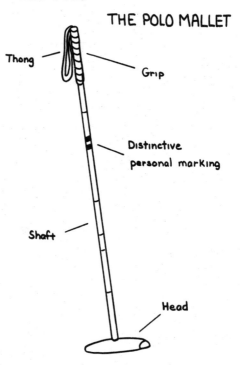

Thong

Grip

Distinctive
personal marking

Shaft

Head

and, if you have a small horse, a 49-inch one.

Mallets also vary in terms of the flexibility of the shaft; you may prefer a whippy or a stiff mallet. Short-jointed cane is relatively stiff, while cane with longer joints is whippier. While the whippiness of a mallet is a matter of individual preference learned from experience, beginners will find it best to use a relatively stiff mallet. This serves better for poke shots, short passes, and shots for goal, and for the inexperienced player it is easier to handle and easier to swing with accuracy. The whippy mallet can drive the ball farther when the same force is used, but its effective use requires more skill.

Rose State College Library

Polo mallets of different lengths, including a practice mallet

The conventional cigar shaped mallet head (slightly tapered at both ends) usually measures nine-and-one-quarter by one-and-one-half inches. Other shapes are used, however, although infrequently. A few have the same diameter

34370

Mallet head

throughout, a few are curved upward at the ends. As a beginner it is best to stay with the conventional design.

Some players like a relatively large (thick) grip, others prefer a small (thin) one. The length and width of the player's hand is an important consideration, but the choice of grip is largely a matter of individual "feel." Whatever is comfortable is right. If the grip on the mallet is too thin, it may easily be wrapped with adhesive tape (or insulating tape) to the bulk desired.

The thong must be long enough to be wrapped around the thumb and passed over the back of the hand. If the thong is long, you twist it several times around your thumb; it is difficult to find a thong too short to enclose the thumb and be passed over the back of the hand. The manner of wrapping the thong around your thumb and hand is covered in Chapter Eight.

After a time, the thong is sure to break at either side, where it is attached to the grip of the mallet. When this occurs, cut off the frayed (broken) end with scissors, tack it on to the slightly protruding upper rim of the grip with a small two-pronged staple, and cover it with black adhesive (insulating) tape.

It is well to identify your mallets; not that another player or anyone else would deliberately steal one, but after a game —when everyone is hot and tired and wanting to take a shower and hurry to the after-game social amenities, and gathers up a bundle of mallets—yours might accidentally be included in someone else's bundle. Two distinctive and easy ways of identifying your mallet are: 1) Print your last name, nickname, or initials on the top of the grip which generally and obligingly is covered with white leather. 2) Place two or three rings of plastic colored adhesive tape on the shaft— above the end winding near the head and again about midway up the shaft. You may use one or a combination of colors. Another, slightly more costly, means of identifying your mallet is to *stamp* your initials on the top of the head.

It is good to have a short "wrist strengthener" mallet 1) to get your wrist and forearm in shape before the polo season begins and 2) to keep your arm in shape during the season.

Distinctive markings on the mallet shaft

Name on top of mallet grip

5
THE FIELD

A full-sized polo field requires about 15 to 20 acres of level ground. The playing surface is actually 300 yards long and 160 yards wide, but of course there must be a substantial area behind the goal posts at each end and along and beyond the side boards on each side. There must be picket lines for the horses; and a stable and club room are desirable.

The field must be well drained, seeded to grow tough, light turf, regularly watered, weeded and cut short; divots need to be replaced after every game—and some after every period. Six hundred yards of side board (ten inches high) must be placed and maintained along the two long sides of the field. While a boarded field is more satisfactory and generally used, polo may be, and sometimes is, played on an unboarded field. When there are no sideboards, the field is 200 yards wide instead of the boarded 160. Goal posts must be placed and maintained 24 feet apart.

Building and maintaining a polo field is expensive. Here are some detailed specifications:

Length: 300 yards from back line to back line, running north and south if practicable.

Width: 160 yards.

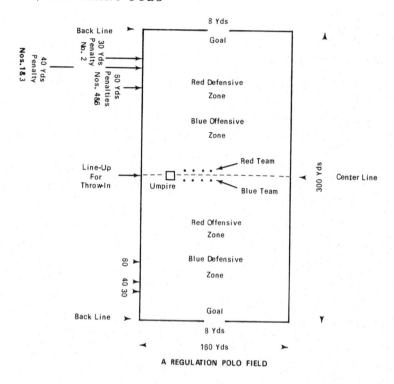

A REGULATION POLO FIELD

Sideboards: 10 inches high by an inch or three-quarter inch thick and 12 feet long.

Goal posts: 10 feet high and 8 yards apart, constructed of light slats covered with canvas, round, uniform throughout and generally 12 inches in diameter. They are placed at both ends of the field.

Footing (ground cover): This depends, understandably, on where the field is located. It must be tough, easily maintained, and long lasting. Landscape gardening firms and the grounds managers of golf courses can suggest the type of grass or grasses to seed.

A full-sized field has to be kept in well-groomed "billiard table" condition so that the small heavy wooden ball can be hit (this would be difficult in high grass or on a rough field with depressions into which the ball might fall) and so that it will roll. Such a field is expensive to construct and expensive to maintain. But the beginner doesn't need this kind of polo field. By using an indoor or arena type inflated ball or a toy hollow rubber ball, you can practice and play (with three instead of four on a side) on a much smaller and rougher field.

A *paddock polo field* is relatively inexpensive to construct and maintain—provided two or three acres of relatively level grassland are available. If the stones are removed from it and it is cut with a gang-mower it will provide a suitable surface for hitting the inflated "indoor" ball, which tends to "float" on the relatively rough surface (as compared to that of the groomed full-size field).

The best size for a paddock polo field is 100 to 150 yards long by 40 to 60 yeards wide. The long axis should lie as nearly as practicable north and south.

Goal posts at each end of a paddock polo field are set ten feet apart and made of two-inch poles painted white. The poles should project eight feet above the ground and rest in sections of lead pipe, which are closed and pointed at one end (the local welding, machine, or automotive shop can do this), two-and-one-quarter inches in diameter, and driven two feet into the ground and flush with it. When the goal posts are removed from the pipe a two-and-one-half-foot length of two-and-one-eighth-inch pole is placed in the pipe to keep foreign matter out. Small pennants, about twelve inches long and eight inches wide at the base, are attached (with strong thumb tacks) to the top of each goal pole.

The best side boards are made of standard ten-by-three-quarter-inch boards cut to twelve foot lengths. For a 100 yard field, you will need 50 of them, 25 on each side. On each twelve foot board, you will need two iron (or other rigid metal) strips, one-eighth-inch thick, one inch wide and sixteen inches long, pointed at one end and with two screw holes to hold the board upright. Eight inches of the metal strip are screwed to the board while eight inches (the pointed end) are in the ground.

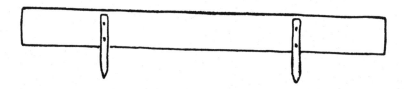

Again a local farrier or machinist can make the metal strips. You will, it is obvious, need 50 times 2, or 100 of them. The boards are usually painted white or red. To enclose a paddock polo field, two-inch-by-two-inch rails, or poles two inches in diameter and ten or twelve feet long, may be inserted in hollow cinderblock and substituted for regulation side boards. Scrapped railroad ties also make acceptable side boards; frequently they may be obtained at no cost.

You may wish to provide a practice area off the field if sufficient ground is available. And you may wish to construct a couple of "wooden horses" for hitting practice. This training facility, which is inexpensive and easy to make, is described in Chapter Eight.

A dozen or so rubber pylons, such as are used to mark off highway construction, set in a line six to eight feet apart, make an excellent training aid for handiness. This is called a *bending course.* You gallop around, or in and out of, the cones in a continuous serpentine. The closer you ride to the cone (that is, the "tighter" the turns), the better your horse does. The horse should, of course, execute a flying change of lead at each turn.

A polo arena differs from a paddock polo field in that the playing surface is enclosed by *knee boards* about four feet high, and goal posts are replaced by a solid goal area (back-board) at each end, against which the inflated ball is hit to score a goal. The arena may be covered (indoor polo) or open (arena polo).

An outdoor arena

A large indoor arena, the Squadron A Armory in New York

A medium-sized indoor arena at Shallow Brook, Connecticut

A paddock polo field at Hidden Hill, Keswick, Virginia

6
WHAT YOU NEED TO START

To start playing polo, you will need to have or acquire:
A suitable mount
Appropriate tack and equipment for your horse
A polo cap and appropriate clothes (See Chapter 15)
A field in which to practice "stick and ball"
An area in which to school your horse
Several practice balls
A couple of polo mallets
The latest United States Polo Association's Year Book, which contains the rules, a list of players with their handicaps, and interesting reference material
An acquaintance or friend who is an experienced polo player—regardless of his handicap (rating)
All of the above, except the practice balls, are discussed in succeeding chapters.

You will want, eventually, to have one or two regulation indoor balls. To start, however, it is well to purchase half a dozen children's hollow rubber balls of the proper size, as described in Chapter Three.

7
YOUR MOUNT

WHAT YOU NEED:

Your mount, while you are a beginner, needs to be:

Quiet. Calm and well mannered.

Experienced. Your mount should have been already used as a polo mount for several years. This way, only *you* will have to learn the game.

Handy. He should be able to stop, turn, and change direction easily and promptly.

Sound. That is, *playing* sound. He may have a splint, curb, spavin, bow, or any number of ailments or blemishes as long as they do not interfere materially with his work.

Small. 15.0 to 15.1 hands. It will be easier to hit from a small mount, and he will be handier, hardier, and less expensive to keep than a larger horse. (Later on, you may want to play a horse 15.2 or 15.3 hands in height, but it is best to start with a small one.)

Speed is the ingredient obviously omitted. You won't need it as a beginner. You won't for some time be up to hitting, or even maneuvering, at speed. It is important, as a beginner, to concentrate on hitting the ball accurately and far and

Typical polo mounts

on playing your position—riding promptly to where you ought to be. It is difficult to do these things on a horse that is difficult to manage or that requires a lot of your attention and effort.

A horse that is bold, alert and eager as well as fast is something you will want—and need—later on. But as a beginner it is best to ride a horse that does not himself present problems.

WHERE DO YOU FIND HIM?

The kind of mount described in the preceding section may be found among the "strings" of most experienced players. Almost everyone has a favorite "pony" of an age where he is not fast enough or strong enough for the company in which his owner is playing. Other players find that they have to reduce the number of mounts they are keeping up, and still others want to replace one or more of their mounts with new young horses.

If you are a good horseman, you can sometimes pick up a bargain or a gift in a horse that has some minor vice or bad habit which is not difficult to correct, but which his owner does not have the time or disposition to bother with.

A YOUNG OR GREEN HORSE:

On the other hand, you may be an accomplished horseman now broadening your mounted activities to include polo. Or you may be a breeder interested in raising and schooling your own young stock, in "making" your own polo pony. In this instance, you will want your prospect to show a potential for speed as well as handiness and, in addition, to show promise of boldness and endurance.

Since it is unwise to subject a horse to the rigors of polo

Typical polo mounts

Typical polo mounts

until he is mature (four or, better, five), you will probably want to select from the horses you are breeding a promising four to six year old, already schooled or used for something else, and begin schooling him for polo.

If you purchase a four or five year old to train yourself, you will need to look for some special features of conformation and temperament. You will want your prospective purchase to indicate that he is alert, calm, eager, bold, fast, handy, and rugged. He should be a little short rather than long in the back; have short cannons and good bone; be somewhat wider than narrow in the chest; and have a head and eyes that indicate intelligence. It will help your stroking if your polo mount is not over 15.2 hands; provided he has the other qualities you are looking for, it is better if he is 15.0 or 15.1.

BREEDING:

For beginners, half-thoroughbreds and the "racing" type of quarter horse, by and large, seem to perform best on the polo field. Thoroughbreds often are too "hot" and tend to be fragile; quarter horses are too often not fast enough. (This seems also to be true of Arabians.) However, many thoroughbreds are seen in high goal polo. In color breeds, you must be guided strictly by the aptitude and performance of the individual.

BASIC SCHOOLING:

Getting used to the mallet:

If you don't accustom your mount to carrying you when you have a mallet in hand, he may behave differently when you do and when you don't carry one. Therefore, your initial training should be getting your mount used to your

Mare "Miss Breeze," winner of the U.S.P.A. award for best pony in the Southeastern Circuit Intracircuit 12-goal Tournament in 1967 at Middleburg, Virginia

carrying and swinging a mallet. This becomes a sort of common denominator of all training.

During relaxed walks on trails, country roads, open pasture, and the polo field itself, hold and then slowly and easily swing the mallet on the off and near sides (The *near side*

Getting used to the mallet

of a horse is its left side, the *off side* its right) until your mount does not "spook" and pays no attention to the mallet. Next, from time to time, after swinging the mallet, rub the mallet head along his neck, flank, and rump—on whichever side you swing. Then swing the mallet under his neck from both the off and near sides, then behind the tail from both sides.

Next—when your mount is relaxed and unconcerned about the mallet at a walk—go through the same routine at a trot, and then at a canter. As your horse becomes accustomed to your swinging the mallet, swing it *hard*, both forward and back on each side, and under the neck and tail from both sides.

As you proceed to other phases of training, always carry and swing a mallet. This is essential to your horse's schooling for polo, and it will contribute substantially to conditioning your wrist, arm, and shoulder muscles.

Controlled Canter:

Whether you have an experienced horse or a green one, after he has become used to the mallet the next step in schooling is to teach him to go consistently and easily at a controlled canter several times around the training area and several lengths of it in both directions without pulling and without breaking into a burst of speed. A controlled canter provides relaxation while you are temporarily out of the play during a game, permits you better control of the ball when you are temporarily "alone," and lets you position yourself easily to take advantage of a situation and move in at speed. Having your mount move at a controlled canter will also allow you to get the most out of "stick and ball" practice.

Figures Eight:

Figures eight balance and supple your horse and prepare

him for the quick halts and rapid, sharp turns so much needed on the playing field.

Start by cantering a left-handed circle of about 30 feet in diameter six times. Then canter the same size circle six times to the right. Now canter six figures eight, making two 30-foot circles (one left, then one right, or vice-versa) six times—with flying changes of lead when you change from one to the other circle. As soon as your horse does well on these large circles, repeat the schooling (singly and in figure eights) on circles of 20 feet in diameter, then on circles of 10 feet in diameter. The last is very tight and difficult; it will take time to do it well.

Cantering a tight figure eight is a training necessity and a basic exercise. It should be an element of each day's schooling.

Speed from a Canter:

It is important in order to conserve your mount's energy during a game that he be permitted to relax whenever the situation allows. Your horse will seldom have an opportunity just to stand and walk except when lining up on the center line or before a hit-in. At other times, however, he can be brought down for a moment to a relaxed canter—that is, if you have trained him to break away from a slow canter to a full gallop immediately. This transition is not difficult to achieve, but it does require teaching your horse to respond instantly and smoothly, and it takes continual practice between games to keep him performing this important maneuver at his best.

Speed from a Standstill:

You have heard of players and horses being "left flat-footed." After a rapid change in the direction or development of the play, you may indeed find yourself standing still and deciding in which direction to move to meet the new (and changed) situation. There is little time. You need promptly to break into a full, hard gallop from that temporary halt. To do it promptly and smoothly, your horse must be alert. He can and will be if you spend enough time teaching him how and letting him know what is expected of him. This ability must be practiced and sharpened continuously.

The Abrupt Stop (Halt or Pulling Up):

If one had to pick one ability out of the several a good polo pony must have, it would very likely be the ability to stop instantly and turn.

To acquire this important ability, your horse needs to lighten his forehand and get his hocks well under him, his head bent at the poll. Many—far too many—polo mounts and Western horses come to an abrupt stop on stiff front legs, their muzzles pointed out, completely off balance. Not only is this an ineffective and jarring stop, but it will also soon wear your horse down to uselessness.

In order to teach your horse to halt on his quarters, you must first teach him to halt from a walk with his hocks well under him. This is done by urging him into the bit with your legs, to meet there a restraining hand. When he begins to get his hind legs well under him, teach him to back smoothly and with proper balance in cadenced steps. Now flex and supple your horse by (again, first from a walk) asking him to halt, then immediately to back about six steps and then immediately to move forward again. Next do this from a trot (with the back, of course, executed at the walk—the only natural way it can be done), and then from a slow canter.

When your horse has learned properly to stop abruptly with his hind legs well under him, balanced and ready to spring ahead again at a canter, practice this series of moves (halt, back, move ahead again) at a fast canter and then at a gallop.

Again you will need to work very hard on this one. Make it, along with figures eight, an element of each schooling and exercise session.

Without the ability to stop abruptly on the quarters, you don't have a polo pony.

Sharp Turns and Turns About:

These are essential abilities of a useful polo mount. A necessary prelude to sharp turns in all directions, and about, is a correct abrupt halt with the horse's hind legs well under him. The tight figures eight will also prepare your pony for the sharp turns and turns about. Both the abrupt halt and the figures eight are covered earlier in this chapter.

First, from a standstill, turn your horse on the quarters a quarter turn (90 degrees) to the left, then to the right, then to the left about (180 degrees) and the right about. Be sure he pivots on a hind foot and does not step backward or throw his quarters to the opposite side (causing a wheeling turn).

When these turns have been mastered from a halt, teach your horse to make them from a walk. When the turns are being done properly, willingly, and smoothly from a walk, work on them from an easy canter and then at a gallop.

What is written here on this subject takes little time to read, but it takes a long time and progressive, orderly, and careful training to get a horse to make his turns promptly, effectively, and smoothly—to the great benefit of your game.

Galloping Straight on the Ball:

Once you have accustomed your horse to the mallet and the ball and practiced all the strokes from his back, slowly and at speed, there should be little trouble on this score.

But troubles will develop if you are careless and thoughtless in your riding, your use of the reins, or your use of the mallet.

If you are heavy-handed and pull on your horse's mouth, causing him pain, he will concentrate on fighting the bit and ignore your legs and the shift of your weight to the point that he will gallop straight ahead and overrun or veer away from (shy off) the ball.

If you hold on to your horse's mouth as you stroke (instead of moving your left hand forward when you hit), he will counter your bad treatment by slowing up, stopping, or shying away from the ball.

Many horses also develop the disconcerting habit of anticipating back shots on both sides. This is not a vice, and it is not due to any mistreatment or carelessness on the part of the rider. It is the learned response of an intelligent horse. The horse has learned that when his rider shifts his weight and position in the saddle to make a back shot (especially a nearside back shot) he will almost immediately be asked to turn about. Having learned this, your horse turns, anticipating your next move or request. The trouble is that your horse does this too soon and ruins your stroke by placing you in a position from which you can't hit the ball.

What can you do about this? You will have to spend many hours swinging your mallet as for a back shot and, with a whip and spurs, urging your horse on for several strides before you use the rein and leg aids to turn. Sooner or later your horse will catch on and turn only when you give the rein and leg aids.

Slow cantering practice at "stick and ball," using all of the eight strokes, and much dribbling in circles will do more than anything else to keep your horse straight on the ball.

Riding Off:

Riding off is a maneuver whereby an opponent's effort is

neutralized by your riding next to him and pushing him out of position—so that you can hit the ball, spoil his attempt to hit it, or block him from interfering with one of your teammates. Schooling in riding off requires a mounted assistant, who need not be a polo player. The object of schooling in this ability is to develop in your horse the willingness to ride off and confidence in his ability to do so.

First at a walk and then at an easy canter, have your horse ride shoulder to shoulder next to another horse. Then, again at a walk and then a canter, ride next to the other horse with your horse's shoulder in *front* of the other horse's shoulder and easily but surely push the other horse away from you. That is, ride off the other horse. Do this about ten times each schooling session for at least a week.

When your horse does not hesitate to ride off the other horse—and this should be accomplished with assurance by the end of a week—start from *behind* and at a little distance away to ride off your assistant. Do this from both sides, without leaning out of the saddle or using your elbows.

Instruct your assistant to give way in the early stages with little opposition; as your horse progresses, instruct your assistant to resist to the best of his or her ability. Continue this sort of work (remember, on *both* sides) until your horse is bold and aggressive in riding off. The secret is to get your horse's shoulder *ahead* of the other horse's shoulder. Train your horse to do this and he will relish the job—because it pays off!

Meeting:

Again, you need a mounted assistant. The schooling follows the same pattern as for riding off.

First have your mounted assistant ride toward you, his or her mallet straight up, and pass close to you at a walk with a small gap between you on your *off* sides. Then repeat the exercise at a trot, at a slow canter, and finally at a gallop. Next repeat the exercise with mallets down and, as you pass, let the mallet heads meet with a good "clack."

Finally, place a ball on the ground. Your mounted assistant and you should then approach it several times from opposite directions the assistant hitting at it and you hitting it. Do this first at a walk, then repeat it at a slow canter, a fast canter, and then an all-out gallop.

If these exercises are conducted progressively and with discretion, your horse should develop boldness in meeting an opponent and learn to gallop true on the line of the ball.

TRAINING AIDS:

The primary training aids you require are:

1) A flat and reasonably level piece of ground (preferably with grass footing closely mowed), with any kind of posts, pylons or rods 10 feet apart at one end of it to simulate goal posts. A field 60 yards by 20 yards will do—though 100 yards by 40 would be better.

2) A dozen to twenty used regulation wooden polo balls and about six arena size (four-and-one-half-inch diameter and weighing six ounces—or a little larger) toy rubber balls.

3) Half-a-dozen rubber traffic pylons. They are used to mark the center point of a figure eight and the diameter of a circle, to set up a pattern for bending exercises, to designate the limits of a "field," to designate a point for an abrupt halt, and so on.

4) You might also use a backing chute and a right-angled section of fence to help teach your horse to turn on his quarters. And you might also consider a wooded path or country dirt road about two miles long for hacking and relaxation.

Traffic cones arranged for bending

A backing chute

A right-angled fence

DAILY SCHEDULE:

You will need two daily schedules, one for days when you play (including scrimmages), and one for the days when no games of any kind are scheduled. Every seven days there should be one day of complete rest with nothing scheduled, when the horses are only fed and turned out—not even groomed. This day is not likely to be Sunday, which is usually a game day.

On the day of a scheduled match or scrimmage, you would want no other activity. Your horses would remain turned out until brought up for grooming before being loaded for transportation to the polo grounds.

On no-game days—except for your "sabbath"—you would want to follow your schooling (basic and corrective) and exercise schedule. This is best accomplished as early as practicable in the morning, when you and your horses are fresh and keen—and when it is cool. Then, after additional grooming, they would be turned out.

8

THE STROKES AND HITTING

WHAT YOU NEED

To utilize effectively, at a gallop in a game, the eight basic polo strokes (and some modifications of them), you need to learn how properly to execute each of them; therefore, you must spend a great deal of time practicing what you have learned, correcting faults and weaknesses, and refining your technique.

To start learning and practicing, you need these things:

A Mallet:
Detailed characteristics of the mallet and qualities the beginner should consider are covered in Chapter Four.

A Stationary Wooden Practice Horse:
You will start your practice in stroking standing on this. The top of the footboards of the wooden horse should be the same height from the ground as the stirrup tread of the saddle used on your favorite polo mount.

A stationary wooden practice horse

Polo Balls:
You will, of course, need a number of these—regulation wooden ones, and some toy rubber balls or an inflated leather arena ball.

A Shortened Mallet:
This is for practicing stroking and hitting while walking dismounted. You can learn a good deal by using the shortened mallet with a tennis or toy ball—or a regulation wooden ball—while you are taking a walk or during a scheduled period for this specific purpose. Children of polo players are frequently introduced to polo this way.

You use a regular (preferably discarded or broken) mallet shortened to a length which permits you the smooth execution of a forward and back stroke on your right side while

Toy balls, for practice

standing and walking erect. This means that you will have to lean down a little when stroking on your left side.

Backboard:

This is for use with a tennis ball and the shortened mallet. The fore and back strokes on the off and near side can be practiced dismounted with a considerable saving of time and space by hitting a tennis ball against a backboard with a target area marked on it. You may use a regulation wooden ball instead of a tennis ball, but the forceful impact will require a very strong (thick) backboard of heavy wood and a surrounding area that is not easily damaged.

Assuming that you use a tennis ball, the backboard may be made of half-inch board or plywood about eight feet wide by six to eight feet high. It may be held upright by a simply constructed supporting frame, or fastened to the side of a stable, garage, or other outbuilding. Two vertical stripes two feet six inches apart (painted or marked with tape) in the middle of the board designate the target area.

Set up a hitting area ten yards distant from and level with the base of the backboard. This may be the natural ground (dirt or turf) or a section of cocoa mat large enough to stand on and hit from with the shortened mallet. An area about five by four feet is adequate.

This device can be set up outdoors or indoors.

The aim of practicing with the backboard is to hit the tennis ball with a full stroke straight and hard enough from your position ten yards away so that it will strike within the target area of the backboard a foot or two off the ground and bounce back. You face the backboard when making the off and near side forward strokes and face away from it when practicing off and near side back strokes.

You will also want to practice quarter and half strokes. The ball should not rise—or rise only slightly—from the ground, and should hit the backboard in the target area hard enough to bounce back a little way. (A *full* stroke is a stroke in which the mallet is swung from an upright vertical position through an arc of 180 degrees to the ground. A *half* stroke is a stroke in which the mallet is swung from an extended horizontal position through an arc of 90 degrees. A *quarter* stroke is a stroke in which the mallet is swung through an arc of only about 45 degrees.)

A shortened mallet used on foot

A shortened mallet used on a bicycle

Wrist Strengthener:

A helpful device for quickly strengthening your wrist and forearm (and, to some extent, your shoulder) is a shortened mallet with a weighted head. This is constructed by sawing off the head portion of a broken or discarded mallet (easily obtainable from an active player) about 27 inches from the top of the grip—or about four inches from the ground when it is carried with the weighted end down. Put the shortened end into a pound and a half of molten lead (encased in a piece of one-half to two-inch pipe), and fasten this lead weight (about one-and-one-quarter to one-and-one-half pounds) securely to the shortened shaft. The local plumber can do this job for you.

The wrist strengthener

If you like, you may cover the lead bulb on the end of your "strengthener" with leather. Your saddle shop should be able to do this.

The use of the wrist strengthener will be covered later in this chapter.

A Hitting Cage:

If a hitting cage is available to you—most clubs have one—you will find it very helpful in practicing and refining your strokes.

A hitting practice cage

A Suitable Mount:

It should not need saying, but since the precept is so often ignored, I will suggest that you learn how to stroke and hit on a quiet, easy cantering, well-mannered, and experienced pony—if not your own, then a borrowed or hired one. Early learning and practice on a live horse require one that will not shy off or stop on the ball, and one which will maintain an even slow canter with the least attention from you. With such a mount you may concentrate on hitting the ball properly; this is difficult if you are diverted by having to manage your mount.

A GENERAL PLAN FOR LEARNING:

To learn to hit a polo ball effectively (accurately and hard) from a fast galloping horse, certain accepted principles of learning and teaching, which have been established through long and varied experience, must be applied. These are:

1) *Orderly progression* from the fundamental principles through the satisfactory performance of one stroke to another, taking as much time as is needed on each stroke until all have been mastered.

2) *Planned, orderly* practice to perfect the strokes.

I have observed several five day "polo schools" in which brand-new beginners spend a short time on the stationary wooden practice horse without preliminary explanatory instruction even about how to *hold* the mallet, with no indication as to the desired position of the ball when it is struck, and without any practice in hitting the ball from that stationary position. They start by having the ball bowled at them. On the third day of this "practice," the beginners are engaged in a "game," trotting or galloping out of control all over the field—many on strange mounts—improperly holding mallets of improper lengths, missing and hitting badly in every direction, standing on the ball, and in general illustrating almost every known fault of stroking and position play. In their five days they learn only two things—how bad they are and how much there is to learn.

Following is the broad outline of a progressive (and intensive) program of instruction in the eight common polo strokes, some modifications of them, dribbling, and free penalty hits at goal. The program, obviously, requires the guidance and supervision of an experienced polo player.

Outline of Instruction in Stroking and Hitting:

1) Selection of a mallet, paying attention to the correct length, weight, rigidity and grip for the individual concerned.

2) How to hold the mallet, with illustration and practice.

3) How to wrap the thong around thumb and hand, with illustration and practice.

4) Off side forward stroke on the stationary wooden practice horse. Emphasis on timing, outward bend of wrist, point of impact and follow-through.

   a) Stationary ball: one-quarter stroke, one-half stroke, full stroke.

   b) Ball bowled toward student from 45 degrees ahead: one-quarter stroke, one-half stroke, full stroke.

   c) Ball bowled from directly behind student: one-quarter stroke, one-half stroke, full stroke.

5) Off side back stroke on the stationary wooden practice horse. Emphasis on timing, bend of wrist, parallel-to-horse swing, point of impact and follow-through.

   a), b), and c) as in section 4) preceding.

6) Near side back stroke, using the shortened mallet, standing and walking dismounted. Demonstration and practice. Emphasize similarity to off side *forward* stroke, importance of leaning over with shoulders parallel to horse, forward point of impact and follow-through. (This will require turning and walking back and forth to where the ball was hit.)

Practice on stationary wooden horse, with stationary and bowled balls.

7) Near side forward stroke, using the shortened mallet, as in section 6) preceding. Emphasis on similarity to tennis backhand stroke, turn of wrist, parallel-to-horse swing, point of impact and follow-through.

Practice on stationary wooden horse, with stationary and bowled balls.

8) Mounted practice under the supervision of a coach.

   a) Off side forward stroke.

     First at a walk: one-quarter stroke, one-half stroke, full stroke. Then at a slow canter: one-quarter stroke, one-half stroke, full stroke. Emphasize moving rein hand forward.

   b) Off side back stroke, as in a) preceding.

c) Near side back stroke, as in a) preceding.

d) Near side forward stroke, as in a) preceding.

9) Under-the-neck strokes, mounted. From the off and near sides.

a) Standing still.

b) At a walk.

c) At a slow canter.

10) Under-the-tail strokes, mounted. From the off and near sides.

a), b), and c) as in section 9) preceding.

11) Slice and cut strokes.

a) With the shortened mallet, dismounted. First standing still and then walking, right side only. (Have an experienced player to demonstrate and coach.)

b) Mounted, off side only. From a standstill, walk, and slow canter.

12) Dribbling, mounted, at a slow canter.

a) Straight ahead, length of field (off side).

b) Straight ahead, length of field (near side).

c) In a large circle, right handed.

d) In as small a circle as practicable, right handed.

e) In a large circle, left handed.

f) In as small a circle as practicable, left handed.

13) Free penalty hits at goal, mounted.

a) From 30 yards, at a walk: one-half stroke.

b) From 40 yards, at a slow canter: full stroke.

c) From 60 yards, at a canter: full stroke.

A lot of detail, a long time? Yes! But if you want to learn how to hit a polo ball effectively, this is what it takes.

HOLDING THE MALLET

The mallet is held with all fingers of the right hand around the top end of the grip—much as one would hold a tennis racket. The thumb lies along the grip to meet the index finger. The knob on the top of the grip rests on the left bulb of the hand below the wrist. The shaft of the mallet is held in such a way that, when the forearm is extended, the ball will be hit with the long side of the head (which is slanted to rest evenly on the ground) where the shaft enters it. The ball is *not* hit with the point of the mallet head.

Normally, the mallet is held in the right hand. You *can* hold the mallet in the left hand—which, of course, is what you would like to do if you are left-handed. Unless, however, you have had a lot of experience in good company, playing left-handed is very dangerous to you and to all of the others on the field. For, even if you hold the mallet in your left hand, you will have to place yourself with respect to the ball *as if you were right handed,* thus making from the off side of your mount what is in effect a near side stroke for a right hander. (See Chapter Ten.) If you can learn to use the mallet in your right hand, it will pay big dividends and avoid much misery.

After you have learned how to hold the mallet correctly— and this should be accomplished after a few attempts—you will need to learn how to use the thong attached to the upper end of the grip. This is designed to avoid losing the mallet if you lose your grip on it. The fabric thong also provides some support since it passes tightly over the back of the hand.

The thong is wound around the thumb and then looped over the back of the hand. In no case should you pass your hand through the thong so that it encircles your wrist; by doing so, you risk being dragged off your horse.

Adjustment of the mallet thong

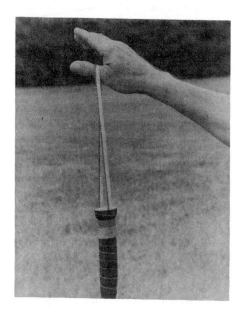

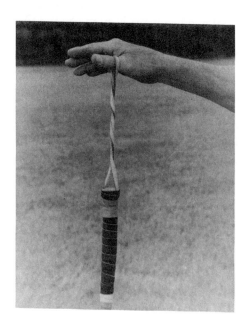

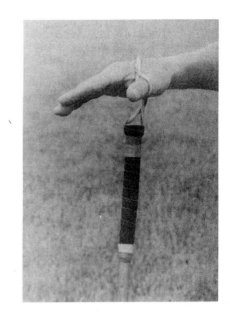

GENERAL COMMENTS ON THE STROKES

The essence of good stroking is to:
a) keep your wrist turned so that the arc of your stroke is parallel to your mount; b) hesitate momentarily at the top, or beginning, of the stroke to assure correct timing; c) keep your eye on the ball; d) hit the ball as it lies in a position—usually a little ahead of your stirrup opposite the horse's shoulder—which will result in the stroke being most effective; e) follow-through; f) move your left (rein) hand forward as you stroke so as not to pull on your horse's mouth as you hit; and g) start your strokes by moving your shoulders parallel to your horse's spine.

Mistakes, difficulties, and ineffective hitting result, obviously, from a failure to follow the above precepts. There is another—quite natural—fault: trying too hard to hit too hard!

You must also learn to use the stroke best suited to the situation. An experienced player knows when to dribble, when to hit a short pass, and when to slam it hard down the field; when to change from the near side to the off side and vice versa; when to hit laterally under the neck to turn the play, and when to back to a teammate. Obviously, all this requires skillful use of the mallet, and the ability to execute confidently all of the strokes.

In the following paragraphs you will read repeatedly "shoulders parallel to the horse's spine" and "swinging in an arc parallel to the horse's spine." These mean that your seat must be out of the saddle, your weight supported largely by the stirrup irons, and that your knees and feet must turn with your right shoulder. For example, in making the off side forward stroke, the right shoulder is brought back and the left shoulder forward so that the line of the shoulders is parallel to the horse's spine. At the same time, the left knee and left foot are turned toward the right (the knee into the saddle), and the right knee and foot turned outward to the right.

Position Of The Ball
for the eight basic strokes

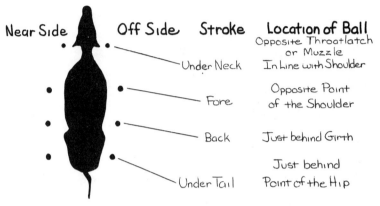

Near Side	Off Side	Stroke	Location of Ball
			Opposite Throatlatch or Muzzle
		Under Neck	In Line with Shoulder
		Fore	Opposite Point of the Shoulder
		Back	Just behind Girth
		Under Tail	Just behind Point of the Hip

Position of the ball for the eight basic strokes

As in golf, you must not push or press, and you must not use undue force on the down swing before connecting with the ball. The weight of the mallet head will provide all of the momentum and force needed here. Apply a slight wrist snap on impact—and apply force to the follow-through.

THE "REST POSITION"

When not actually stroking or attempting to "hook" an opponent's mallet, the mallet is held in the "rest position." The mallet head is up and the shaft is perpendicular to the forearm which, in turn, is at a right angle to the upper arm. The mallet is balanced and the player's wrist, hand, and arm are relaxed.

The rest position

OFF SIDE FORWARD STROKE

During a game, about 75 percent of your strokes will be off side fore strokes. Normally the ball should be hit hard and straight in the direction you are galloping, although sometimes you will want to "slice" the ball to the right or "cut" it to the left.

The important factors in developing an effective off side fore stroke are largely identical to those factors important for improved stroking generally:

1) Swinging in a plane *parallel* to your horse. This is accomplished by bringing the right shoulder back (so that the line of your shoulders is parallel to your horse's spine) and turning the wrist outward.

2) Starting the stroke by bringing the mallet from the "rest position" straight back and *hesitating momentarily* in the starting position. This facilitates correct timing and helps use the weight of the mallet head to the greatest advantage.

3) Using the weight of the mallet head in the downward swing—and not interfering with it by any undue force of the arm (trying too hard to hit too hard).

4) Using the strength of your arm to follow-through forcefully as the force of the mallet head's downward swing is expended.

5) Keeping the wrist out and slightly back until impact (to provide a snap as the wrist straightens), and then holding the wrist straight as the forearm is extended, to assure that the ball will travel straight.

6) Hitting the ball when it is about opposite your horse's shoulder.

It is most important, when mounted, to move your left (rein) hand forward as you stroke. This will both prevent your horse from stopping on the ball and encourage him to move at it boldly. (If you miss the ball, go on!)

Off side forward stroke

The test of a good off side fore shot is good distance, desired direction, and ease.

All of the foregoing, obviously, requires much practice— first on a wooden horse, then walking with a short mallet, then on a schooled horse standing, walking, at a slow canter, at a fast canter, and then at a gallop.

OFF SIDE BACK STROKE

First shift the mallet grip a little to the right. Start the swing by moving your right arm forward from the rest position with your shoulders at a right angle to the horse's spine (your normal riding position). You then swing the mallet backward in an arc parallel to your horse's spine, letting your shoulders turn to a position parallel to your horse's spine, and strike the ball just in front of your horse's hip (well back, compared with the forward stroke) with a wrist snap and good follow-through. Be careful to relax your left (rein) hand to avoid jabbing your horse in the mouth as you hit.

Hitting the ball too soon—that is, when it lies opposite your horse's shoulder or opposite your stirrup—will drive it into the ground instead of backward.

Off side back stroke

NEAR SIDE BACK STROKE

This stroke is similar to the off side forward stroke. The point of impact with the ball is a little forward of the stirrup, or between the stirrup and the horse's shoulder. As with the strokes on the off side, you swing in an arc parallel to the horse's spine and turn your shoulders parallel to it. From the rest position, you move the mallet well over to the left and a little forward to start the stroke. Again be sure not to pull back on the reins as you swing.

Near side back stroke

NEAR SIDE FORWARD STROKE

Shift your grip a little to the right (similar to the slight shift in the off side back stroke) as you bring the mallet well over to the left and back to cover your left shoulder. You then start the swing in a parallel arc with your shoulders parallel to the horse's spine. The point of impact with the ball is at about at your horse's shoulder. Again relax your left hand and do not pull as you swing.

Near side forward stroke

UNDER-THE-NECK STROKE FROM THE OFF SIDE

This stroke is used to hit the ball at a right angle, or nearly right angle, to the left of the direction you are moving; it is frequently used to save or clear a goal, to turn the play, and to pass laterally.

You lean well forward out of the saddle and, with a half to three-quarter swing at a right angle to the horse's spine, hit the ball as it lies or rolls a little to the right of and under your horse's throatlatch or muzzle. The follow-through will bring the mallet head up on the left side of the horse's neck.

Under the neck from the off side

UNDER-THE-NECK STROKE FROM THE NEAR SIDE

This stroke is used for the same purposes as the under-the-neck stroke from the off side but, of course, it moves the ball in the opposite direction (to the right of the direction you are moving).

The stroke is executed like the under-the-neck stroke from the off side, except that it is started on the near side, a little further forward than the near side forward stroke. The point of impact with the ball is a little to the left of and under the throatlatch or muzzle of the horse. This is a difficult stroke which requires much practice.

Under the neck from the near side

UNDER-THE-TAIL STROKES

These strokes (which may be executed from the off and near sides) are only slight modifications of the off side back stroke and the near side back stroke. In each case the point of impact with the ball is further to the rear and the mallet head is angled to direct the ball respectively as much as possible to the left (from the off side) and to the right (from the near side) instead of straight to the rear.

THE "SLICE"

This stroke is used to hit the ball on the off side in a direction from 20 to 50 degrees to the *right* of the direction in which you are riding.

It is accomplished by "slicing" or drawing the mallet head across the ball with the wrist and mallet head turned slightly toward the right (instead of hitting it squarely straight ahead). Otherwise the swing is the same as the one you would use in making an off side forward stroke. This is a difficult stroke which requires much practice.

A slice on the near side (from a near side forward stroke) can be executed but it is extremely difficult and very seldom called for. Probably the time and effort required to master this stroke would be used to greater advantage in improving the more commonly used strokes.

THE "CUT"

This stroke is used to hit the ball from the off side in a direction from 10 to 40 degrees to the *left* of the direction in which you are riding.

It is a stroke between the off side forward and the under-the-neck stroke from the off side. The point of impact with the ball is further forward than the regular off side forward stroke and not as far forward as the under-the-neck stroke. The impact with the ball is just ahead of the right forefoot and is directed to the left front. The mallet head is angled slightly to the left and the arc of the swing is slightly to the left instead of being parallel to the horse's spine—but it does not actually reach under the horse's neck.

This stroke can also be executed from the near side but, for the same reasons noted above about the near side slice, there appears to be little benefit in mastering it. Furthermore, a common fault in learning to execute the difficult near side forward stroke is hitting the ball to the right instead of straight ahead (from a failure to turn the wrist and to swing in an arc parallel to the horse's spine). Trying to hit to the right from the near side might make it a lot harder to hit straight ahead—a feat more often required.

DRIBBLING

The dribble is a succession of short eighth to quarter strokes which roll the ball a short distance on the ground. It is a most effective maneuver when meeting, for extricating the ball from a melee, for starting a "dead" ball on its way preliminary to slamming a long shot down field, when an opponent's hook is imminent and for scoring when you are a short distance from goal. How many good opportunities to score and advance have been lost by taking a full swing at the ball when it should have been dribbled!

Soccer, ice hockey, and basketball provide good examples of the effectiveness of dribbling. And the maneuver is somewhat like a bunt in baseball.

Development of the ability to dribble effectively requires a great deal of practice—both straight ahead and in circles on both sides. It is, understandably, much easier to become reasonably adept at dribbling on the off side than on the near side. You need, therefore, to practice two to three times as long on the near side as you do on the off side.

The dribble is usually executed at the canter and occasionally at a relatively slow gallop; it is, of course, frequently begun at a standstill or a walk.

The left (rein) hand is, as in other strokes, relaxed as you hit the ball.

FREE HITS AT GOAL

The two major penalties, free hits from, respectively, 30 and 40 yards away with all of the opponents behind the back

Dribbling

line and none within the goal area, present excellent opportunities to score. A good team will include a player who can be relied upon to score on nearly all of these penalty hits. Basketball teams have their expert foul shooters and football teams their place-kickers for points after touchdown and field goals; so too in polo, except that in polo you cannot substitute a player to make the free hit. It is a shame in a polo game—as it is on the football field and basketball court —to miss a free try for a score.

In polo, however, it is relatively easy for every player to become adept at scoring when a free hit penalty is awarded by the umpire. It is easy, that is, if he has mastered the basic off side forward stroke, does not try too hard, and relaxes.

The 30-yard penalty hit may be made easily from a walk with a half stroke, the 40-yard penalty hit from a slow canter, using a half or a full stroke. All polo players should practice these shots until they can score nine out of ten tries in practice—and then overcome their nervousness ("buck fever") in a game.

The free penalty hit from 60 yards out, with opponents between the goal posts and in various positions as close as 30 yards to you, is much more difficult than the other two. The 60-yard hit requires a good canter and a strong (and straight) full stroke which will lift the ball over the heads of the opponents. A lot of practice will help you master it.

HOOKING

"Hooking" is used to interfere with, thus spoil, an opponent's attempt to hit the ball by engaging his mallet before his stroke is completed. The rules permit hooking an opponent's mallet only from directly behind and on the side he is stroking—and only when he is attempting to hit the ball.

The United States Polo Association rules cover in considerable detail the definitions of fair and foul hooks, and the penalties for foul hooks; you should become thoroughly familiar with them. Remember especially that you are not permitted to reach over an opponent's mount nor across the mount's legs.

Your mallet head engages the opponent's mallet head as he nears the *bottom* of his swing. Reach out to do this or hold your mallet still, but do not slash at your opponent's mallet. If you do slash at it, you are likely to miss and also break *your* mallet shaft.

PRACTICE

Skillful use of the mallet is essential to playing polo well

Hooking

and, therefore, to enjoying the game. No matter how good your mount, nor how well you ride, nor how much you know about team play, if you cannot hit reliably, you are of little value to a team.

Skillful use of the mallet (for reasonably well-coordinated individuals) requires only a lot of practice under the guidance of a perceptive and knowledgeable coach. The practice, in turn, requires a plan, progressive mastery of each stroke before attempting the next one, concentration on faults and difficulties, and strict attention to your coach's advice.

Further comments on practice and on the use of the "wrist strengthener" will be found in Chapter Twelve.

Who's going to get it? Or did both miss it?

9
HANDICAPS

With a view to reasonably equalizing competition in match games and tournament play, each polo player is assigned in individual handicap by the Handicap Committee of the United States Polo Association. The individual handicaps—ranging from 1 to 10 goals—are published annually in the Association's Year Book.

A player's handicap is based on his ability and experience. Beginners and the inexperienced are rated −1 or 0; two or three are rated ten; about ten each year are assigned handicaps of seven and over; about three percent are rated five or more; approximately half to sixty percent are rated zero. (There are about 1,000 players listed in the Polo Association Year Book.)

Unless the Committee has seen the player in match or tournament play or knows him by reputation, the handicap is based on the recommendations of the club secretary and of a local committee. This generally applies to beginners, inexperienced, casual, and infrequent players.

Since a player's demonstrated ability on the field is the primary basis of his handicap, it is evident that in addition to his hitting and team play, the quality of the mounts he rides will have a marked influence on it.

Individual handicaps are totaled to provide a team handicap. In a match game, the team with the higher total handicap "gives" the team with the lower handicap the difference between the two total handicaps. For example: The four players on the Bluebirds team have handicaps of 0, 2, 3, and 4 respectively, a total team handicap of 9. Players on the Blackhawks team are handicapped respectively at 0, 1, 2, and 3, a total handicap of 6. Therefore the score at the beginning of the game is: Blackhawks 3, Bluebirds 0.

A situation might be imagined in which a 24-goal team is matched against a team of two really good zero players (whose handicaps will probably soon be increased), a very good 2-goal player, and an exceptionally good 3-goal player (whose handicap might also be raised in the next year's list)—and all very well mounted. This would pit a 24-goal team against a 5-goal team with a handicap difference of 19. It is very doubtful the 24 goal team could overcome this handicap. The Polo Association recognizes this. Therefore, tournaments are set up within limits: in any match, tournament or not, the Association rules provide that no team shall be required to concede more than 5 goals!

An additional procedure to equalize play is to conduct tournaments with limitations on the participating teams' handicaps—there are, for example, 6 goal, 10 goal, 12 goal, 16 goal, 20 goal tournaments. (Here again, a team does not concede more than 5 goals.) In a 6 goal tournament, no team may have a team handicap exceeding 6 goals. A team in this tournament may, however, be composed of one 6 goal player and three 0 players.

From the foregoing, two things are evident. First, a player's handicap is indeed a handicap. Second, the most valuable player on a low goal team—perhaps on any team—is a very good zero handicap player.

10
THE RULES AND PENALTIES

CONCEPT

Polo is played at a gallop. The play changes instantly. A player rides hard following the line taken by the ball he has just hit; he is intent on hitting it again toward the opponent's goal. An opponent tries to catch him and ride him off. A teammate is near the opponent's goal waiting for a pass. The opposing back gets into position to turn the play. And, instantly, the situation changes.

The rules of polo—the framework within which the game is played—are designed to assure that the game can be played at speed with safety. If an opponent rides across the line of the ball a player is following, or if he stands over the ball, the player galloping on the line of the ball has an unfortunate choice: he may continue to gallop at speed and cause a bad collision from which both horses and riders may suffer severe injury; or he may check (stop or slow down) to avoid just such a collision. Either action is, of course, undesirable, so the United States Polo Association rules provide that an opponent who crosses the line of the ball commits a foul to be penalized by permitting the fouled side a free hit at the fouling side's (opponent's) goal—from a variety of distances from the goal, depending on where the foul occurred and its severity.

FOULS

Fouls are violations of 11 specified Field Rules of the United States Polo Association. (There are 24 Field Rules in all.) Fouls fall into three broad categories:

1) Actions which interfere with the player galloping toward the ball at speed, who should have the "right" to hit it. These are: crossing the line of the ball, failure to maintain proper position or action when opponents are riding toward the ball either in the same direction or in opposite directions, and improperly standing or turning on the ball.
   Note that in all of the above the distance between players is a factor. Improper action of the kind mentioned above is a foul only when the cross, standing, turning, or meeting is at such a distance that the player "on line of the ball" would have to check or materially reduce his speed in order to avoid a collision.
2) Personal fouls. These include unnecessarily rough bumping, the use of elbows against another player, dangerous hooking of an opponent's mallet by reaching over or in front of his mount (which may cause it to trip or stumble), and striking an opponent or his mount with a mallet or whip.
3) "Technical" fouls, such as hitting the ball behind your own goal line (a safety), and certain infractions of the rules involving the number of players on a side, horse equipment, handicaps and so on.

PENALTIES

There are six penalties involving a free hit at goal (from

distances of 30, 40, and 60 yards, and from the spot where the foul occurred), including the award outright of a goal to the side fouled. Others include: Expulsion of a player on the fouling side for disabling another player, or for deliberate and dangerous fouls and conduct prejudicial to the game; the ordering of a pony off the field because of improper (dangerous) horseshoes or because it has already played on an eliminated team; and the forfeiture of a match.

CROSSING

Since crossing the line of the ball (crossing in front of the player who has the right-of-way close enough to cause him to reduce his speed) is the foul most frequently called, the least understood, and, for both of these reasons, the most often contested, some comments on it appear justified and may prove helpful.

"The line of the ball" is specifically defined as the exact direction the ball is travelling as a result of being hit by the last player who hit it. If the ball is hit straight ahead or at only a slight angle, then the player who last hit the ball and rides on that line for an *offside* stroke has the right-of-way as against anyone entering the line of the ball thus established. But he shares this right of way with 1) an opponent entering or riding on the same line with the ball on his near side, 2) an opponent galloping *toward* him on the same line with the ball on his *off side,* and 3) a player *entering* on the line with the ball on his off side but far enough ahead so that the first player does not have to slow his pace.

With respect to the line of the ball, *left-handed* players must enter and gallop on the line of the ball as if they were right handed. The off (or near) side of the *horse* is the controlling and determining factor in judging correct action and

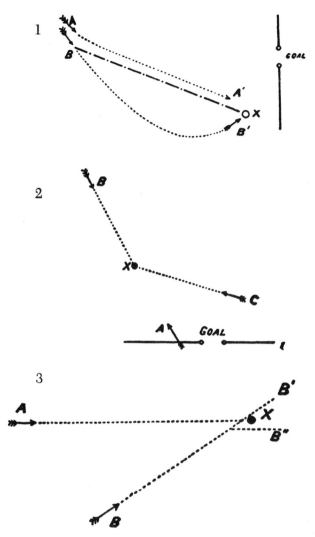

The right of way

(1) A has the right of way. Even though B hit the ball last, he has deviated from the line of the ball while A is riding closely parallel to it.

(2) B has the right of way. B is on the line the ball is traveling, even though he is going in the opposite direction. C would cross the line of the ball.

(3) A has the right of way unless B turns in the direction B″ and hits a near side back shot. If, however, B is at a sufficient distance from A to continue on the line B′ without causing A to reduce the speed at which he is galloping, there is no crossing foul.

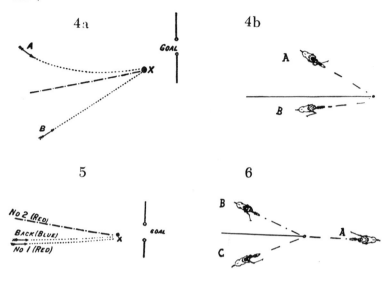

The right of way

(4) a. A has the right of way, since he is riding at less of an angle to the line the ball is traveling and is, therefore, more closely following its line.

(4) b. B, since he is riding at less of an angle to the line the ball is traveling, has the right of way.

(5) No. 2 (Red) has the right of way. If No. 1 (Red) causes the Back (Blue) to cross No. 2 (Red) or to pull up to avoid a collision with him, a dangerous foul would be called against No. 1 (Red)

(6) A has the right of way, but he must hit from the off side. (If B can straighten out and avoid crossing A, he can attempt an off side stroke.) C cannot get into the play without fouling.

the commission of a foul. This means that a left-handed player riding with the line of the ball on his right will have to make what amounts for a right-handed player to a near side forward shot.

"The line of the ball," then, is the direction of the line the ball is travelling when last hit. (This is important and so stated in the rules.) The player riding on that line or at the least angle to it has the right of way. (There are some exceptions and variations when players are riding in opposite directions on or at an angle to the line of the ball: see the United States Polo Association Field Rules.)

At each moment during the game there exists a "line of the ball" and a "right-of-way." A player may not *cross* another player who has the right of way nor enter into the right-of-way (line of the ball) except at a distance which does not involve the possibility of collision or danger to another player. The right-of-way gives a player the right to hit the ball on the *off side* of his mount (whether he is right- or left-handed).

The rules concerning the right-of-way and penalties for crossing are set forth in considerable detail in the United States Polo Association's Field Rule Number 16 and, for arena polo, in Field Rule Number 18. It is important to study and remember them—and, most important, to play in accordance with them for your own safety and popularity.

Diagrams illustrating the application of the rules in five typical situations involving the right-of-way, taken from the United States Polo Association's 1972 Year Book, are shown in diagrams on pages 121 and 122.

11
TEAM PLAY

Since the object of the game of polo is for a team to score more goals than the opposing team, the basic aims of play are for your side to score at every opportunity, to set up the opportunity frequently, and to prevent the opposing team from scoring.

This means that you need an offensive strategy and a plan for each common offensive situation, and a defensive strategy and a plan for each common defensive situation. Some will tell you this is impractical, even impossible, because the game is so fast-moving and the situation constantly and quickly changing. This, however, is true also in horse racing, ice hockey, basketball and lacrosse; and successful jockeys, hockey teams, basketball teams and lacrosse teams do have overall strategies as well as specific plans for a variety of anticipated situations. Successful polo teams also have overall strategies, and plans for the usual situations; these are implemented through team play.

Good team play depends, of course, on coordinated effort in accordance with well-understood and simple plans developed ahead of time. It also depends on mutual confidence and much practice. When a plan fails, it is essential that all players analyze the cause, discuss remedies, and proceed on a new course.

The specific elements of good team play (which will be amplified later) are these:

1) A clear understanding of an agreement on the normal responsibilities of each player when he is riding in or near his *normal* position;

2) A clear understanding of and agreement on the responsibilities of each player when he is *out of* his normal position (as to who interchanges with whom);

3) A clear understanding of the differences among the relative positions of the four (or three) players on both *offense* and *defense,* and of the reasons for them;

4) An overall strategy of offense, including an understanding of where the ball is to be hit and passed, who backs up whom, and who rides which opponent out of the play—in addition to an understanding of the relative positions;

5) An overall strategy of defense (as in 4 preceding):

6) Specific plans for the following situations:

   a) The bowl-in at the beginning of the game and after a goal has been scored,

   b) A bowl-in from the sideboards,

   c) A hit-in by your side,

   d) A hit-in by the opponents,

   e) Penalties 2 through 6 when your side has been fouled,

   f) Penalties 2 through 6 when a foul is called against your side,

   g) A melee in front of the goal your team is attacking,

   h) A melee in front of the goal your team is defending,

   i) When the horn sounds, denoting the base time of a period has expired,

   j) When one of your teammates breaks loose and is in the clear, both in your offensive zone and in your defensive zone, and

   k) When an opposing "star" breaks loose and is in the

clear, both in your offensive zone and in your defensive zone.

7) Specific plans for these special situations:
    a) When two players on your side are riding on the line of the ball from opposite directions, fairly close to it,
    b) When a teammate behind you shouts "Leave it!" and
    c) When you find yourself out of position.

Good team play requires that in every situation each member of the team knows what the others are *supposed* to do and has confidence that each will do this. Four well-mounted, skilled mallet men playing as individuals are frequently defeated by four men not so well mounted and not so skilled with the mallet, who play well together as a *team*.

A team composed of a "star," relatively high handicapped player and three weak, inexperienced players—the "star" with the responsibility of "carrying" the team—will often be defeated by a lower handicapped, balanced team who play well together.

Playing as a team means that each player contributes to every situation, that each helps the other, that there is co-ordination among them, and that in every situation each knows where the others are and what he and the others are expected to do. It means much passing, backing up, and *interchange* of position (as against a haphazard *change* of position); the object is to complement each other's efforts rather than interfering with them. This requires studying and understanding team play, sound coaching, practice, and a lot of playing together.

Here is one incident, among many, demonstrating the importance of team play:

An experienced player was watching his son in his first match game—the second round of a low goal tournament.

The boy was well mounted and an excellent horseman. Since he had been hitting tennis and polo balls with a short mallet on foot from the time he was eight years old (he was now fifteen), and, in the last two years, had been hitting off a quiet old pony in "stick and ball" practice and in scrimmages on his father's private field, he was very skillful with the mallet. He had had, however, no instruction in the principles and practice of team play.

Although the boy's team was favored over their equally handicapped opponents, they lost by four goals.

"I don't understand it. I wonder what was wrong?" the father remarked to a polo playing companion watching beside him. "What do you think?"

"Johnny," his father's friend commented, "was playing Number One—or was supposed to be—wasn't he?"

"Yes, that's right, he was Number One."

"Your son was largely responsible for the defeat."

"I thought he did well; he hit the ball at every opportunity, he rode off their Number Two, and he cleared the goal nicely, probably saved a score—remember that one?" the proud father replied.

"Yes, I recall each of those instances—but he was all over the field, almost never where he should have been, which was up front taking passes hit up to him from behind. Johnny hit the ball half a dozen times when a teammate should have and could have done so. And at least five times he was not in position when the ball was hit into his team's goal area. Had he been there—where Number One is supposed to be—he might easily have scored the four goals by which his team lost, and maybe another to win the game, as they were supposed to!"

Here is another incident:

I recall a very successful team which lost its capable Number One shortly before the opening of its season. The captain of the team induced a capable and athletic young horseman, who had never played polo, to take up the game and join his team. The captain spent a lot of time teaching his young recruit to master thoroughly just two strokes—the off side and near side forward strokes with special attention to quarter and half strokes and dribbling.

The captain kept emphasizing to his recruit that he should stay forward toward the goal his team was attacking. He instructed him never—no matter what the circumstances—to drop back beyond the center line and almost never to move further back than the forward *third* of the field. "You just stay up there near the goal," he said. "We'll pass the ball up to you and you hit it in. Dave (Number Two) will take care of the opposing Back."

This paid off handsomely. The recruit's team did a little better than it had the previous season—which had been quite successful—and won two tournaments.

And the recruit Number One scored half the team's impressive tally of goals! All of course, on passes!

THE POSITIONS

Each position has assigned duties, specific responsibilities, in the overall team effort. When you are necessarily and properly out of position—in the area of and assuming the duties of another position—the teammate playing that position should interchange and cover yours. Similarly, when a teammate "comes through" to *your* position, immediately cover *his*.

Number One:
Number One has two primary responsibilities:
1) to stay well forward toward the goal his team is attacking, receive passes, and score goals; and

2) to ride off, cover, trouble and never lose sight of the opponent's Back. He should ride him off vigorously when his team's Number Two or Three "comes through" and avoid the opposing Back with dexterity when a pass comes up to him. When Number One is placed so that he cannot readily interfere with the opposing Back's stroke, he should place himself to take advantage of the opportunity should the Back miss.

Number One will frequently interchange with Number Two, when Two comes through to follow up a hit. In this situation, Number One should back up Number Two in the event he misses or is ridden off by the opposing back.

The opposing Back is Number One's "opposite number."

Number Two:

Number Two is the chief offensive player, the primary attacker. In general, he is the strongest player on the team—the longest hitter, the best mounted, the most active and aggressive. It is his job to score, directly (coming through while Number One rides off the Back) or indirectly (passing up to Number One so that he can score): He continually forces the attack, and therefore has no primary responsibility for defense.

He will interchange with Number One when he (Number Two) goes through to slam home a scoring drive. He will interchange with Number Three if Three comes through; in this case he assumes the defensive duties of Number Three while he remains in that position, but at the earliest opportunity he should change back to his Number Two position and resume the offensive.

Often Number Two will ride off the opposing Number Three when the latter is galloping with the ball.

The opposing Number Three is Number Two's "opposite number."

Number Three:

Number Three's job is partly offensive, partly defensive. He must be a dependable and experienced player—some believe that he (not Number Two) should be the strongest player on the team. He is often referred to as the *pivot*, since he is relied upon to stop and turn the opponent's attack and move his own team into an offensive drive. Number Three's primary responsibility is to feed the ball from defensive territory up to his forwards, Number Two and Number One, and—where it is advantageous—to himself hit the ball through to a score.

On the attack, and after turning the play, he will frequently interchange with Number Two; on other occasions, after feeding the ball up to Number Two, he will back him up.

On defense, Number Three rides off the opposing Number Two, interchanges with and backs up his team's Back and assumes such other defensive duties as the situation presents in the area from the center line rearward to the back line.

His duties may be compared to those of a halfback on a soccer team.

The opposing Number Two is Number Three's "opposite number."

Back (Number Four):

The Back's primary job is defense of the goal against the opponents' attacks. Defense of the goal means not only breaking up and spoiling attacks, but also turning the play and feeding the ball up to the forwards. From deep in his team's defensive area, he will hit the ball forward toward the sideboard to clear the goal; at other times he will hit a long, hard shot straight up the field to his Number Two; occasionally he will pass to Number Three. The point is that the Back's defense is an active one; he uses it to give the attack back to his own team.

From time to time, the Back will find a favorable opportunity—especially when he is in the forward portion of his defensive zone as his teammates press the attack—to gallop on with the ball all the way to a goal. He will also spend some time riding off the opposing Number Two and Number One and taking the ball away from them.

The Back needs to be an especially reliable hitter, particularly adept at both the off side and near side back strokes; his forward strokes should hit the ball hard and long. He needs to be a "heady" player—the more experienced the better.

Since the Back can observe and appraise the play better than anyone else, since he is (or should be, at any rate) an experienced and skilled player, and since he is therefore best suited to direct the play of his teammates, he is very often the captain of his team.

The opposing Number One is the Back's "opposite number." The Back should never let him get between himself and the goal.

Active Defense

Number Three and the Back are attackers in depth; they must feed the ball up to their forwards. And here it is important to recall a general principle. It must be borne in mind constantly that polo is an aggressive game, that you can win only by scoring goals. Defense, therefore, is only temporary; it must be viewed as an opportunity again to resume a vigorous offense.

ELEMENTS OF TEAM PLAY

Following are some broad general guides to good team play, as applied to the individual player:

1) Play your position as it should be played.

2) Know where your teammates are when you are about to hit.

3) When you are not on the ball, anticipate who will hit it next and where it is *going*, and place yourself accordingly. (Don't *chase* the ball—go to where it is *going*.)

4) Pass whenever there is an opportunity to do so. A pass to a teammate is much more effective than a long shot to an opponent or to nowhere.

5) When a teammate says "Leave it!", do so—and ride off the nearest opponent.

6) Always keep your "opposite number" in view—and evade or cover him as the occasion demands.

7) On the offense, hit toward the goal and look for a pass toward goal.

8) On the defense, hit toward the boards and look for a pass to the sideboards.

9) If you come through another position—or are about to—say "I'm One (Two or Three)" and play that position until the situation changes and you can return to your regular position. Likewise, drop back to cover a teammate coming through you.

10) Don't crowd a teammate. One of you on the ball is enough.

11) Don't say "Leave it!" unless you are sure that you have a better chance to hit effectively than the teammate on the ball.

12) If you are galloping toward the goal your team is attacking and a teammate, riding toward you with his back to the goal and on line of the ball, can *back* it, let him do so; you ride on and pick it up.

13) Do not attempt to turn the play by dribbling the ball in a circle. Instead, *back* it in the direction of a teammate. (Dribbling in a circle during a game is difficult, is very likely to result in a penalty, and may place your teammates out of position.)

14) Don't be a "ball hog."

15) Play for hits rather than misses. Always assume that a teammate or an opponent about to hit the ball *will* hit it for a good average shot; then anticipate where it will go.

16) Remember always that you have teammates, and play a team game.

The team captain needs to direct the players of his team so that at all times there is:

1) Someone in the Number One and Back positions.
2) One teammate *ahead* of the man on the ball and one *behind* him, when your team has possession of the ball.
3) Someone covering the opposing forwards.

USUAL SITUATIONS

Bowl-in:

The principles of team play are substantially the same whether the ball is bowled in at the center line or from the side boards. Which player hits the ball depends largely on how hard and how low the umpire bowls it.

If *Number One* hits the ball, he moves after it for another hit. Numbes Two moves in behind him to back him up. Number Three covers the opposing Two and stays near midfield, alert for an opportunity to press the attack or turn the opponents' hits. The Back gallops back to a defensive position about halfway between the center line and back line and within comfortable distance to ride off the opposing One or Two. See page 134. If an opponent hits the ball, each player covers his opposite number and attempts to turn the play. Number One moves to a position between the opposing Back and the goal he is attacking and stays there to take a pass.

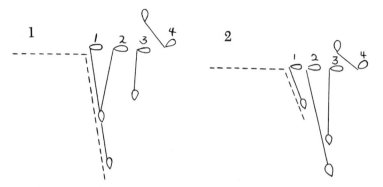

Bowl-in: No. 1 hits the ball. (1) A long hit. No. 2 backs up No. 1. (2) A short hit. No. 1 passes to No. 2, No. 3 backs up No. 2, No. 1 covers No. 3's position.

If *Number Two* hits the ball, he moves after it for another hit. Number One gallops toward goal for a pass. Number Three backs up Number Two. The Back gallops to a defensive position. See below. If an opponent hits the ball, Number Two covers his opposite number, Three.

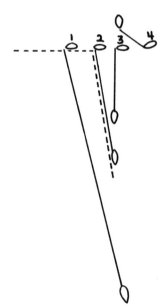

Bowl-in: No. 2 hits the ball. No. 1 gallops toward goal ready to receive a pass, No. 3 backs up No. 2.

If *Number Three* hits the ball, he moves after it for another hit. Number One gallops toward the goal for a pass. Number Two backs up Number Three. The Back gallops to a defensive position. See below. If an opponent hits the ball, Number Three covers his opposite number, Two.

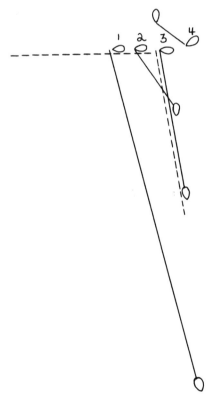

Bowl-in: No. 3 hits the ball. No. 1 gallops toward goal to receive a pass, No. 2 backs up No. 3.

If the *Back* hits the ball, he passes to one of his forwards and moves to a defensive position. One and Two gallop toward goal, One nearer to it than Two, to pick up the Back's pass. Number Three covers the defense (and the opposing One and Two) until the Back can assume these duties, and then returns to his regular position. See below.

If an opponent hits the ball, the Back gallops to a defensive position with the greatest speed, making sure that the opposing Number One does not get ahead of him (between him and the goal).

When the ball is bowled in from the side boards, the same principles of position and team play apply as at the center line, except that all hits and movement on the offense are toward the center of the field.

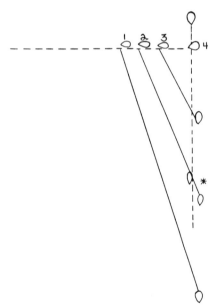

Bowl-in: Back (No. 4) hits the ball. No. 1 gallops toward goal, No. 2 picks up the Back's pass, No. 3 backs up No. 2, Back takes up defensive position. *If the Back hits a long one, No. 2 can take the pass on his off side without the risk of crossing. If the Back hits a short one, No. 2 would take the pass on his near side.

Hit-in from the Back Line:

Generally the ball is hit—hard and long—to the side boards nearest the player hitting in (usually the Back). When a team has a reliable long-hitting Back, has developed sound team play, and is composed of experienced players, two modifications to throw the opponents off balance are warranted.

One is to hit the ball across the defensive goal to the side boards farther from the hitter. The other is for the Back to hit the ball a relatively short distance straight ahead and then to follow up with a long, hard hit straight ahead where his Number Two will gallop to pick it up. Both of these plays require a signal and very rapid movement of the hitter's three teammates away from their "normal" positions near the "near" boards to take advantage of the surprise.

Here we will consider only the "normal" hit-in from the back line to the nearer side boards. Assume the usual: that the Back hits in.

His *Number Two* is near the boards just a little short of where he expects the Back to hit it—ready to carry it along the boards to offensive territory and pass it to Number One.

His *Number One* is about twenty yards from the boards, a little ahead of Number Two, ready to take over in the event the ball is hit beyond Number Two or the latter is heavily covered by opponents. If Number Two does pick up the ball, Number One gallops toward goal ready to receive Number Two's pass.

His *Number Three* takes a position about halfway between the Back and Number Two, ready either to back up Number Two should he miss or be ridden off, or to hit the ball if the Back's hit does not reach Number Two, or to take up the defense if an opponent should turn the play.

The *Back* follows the play in a defensive position.

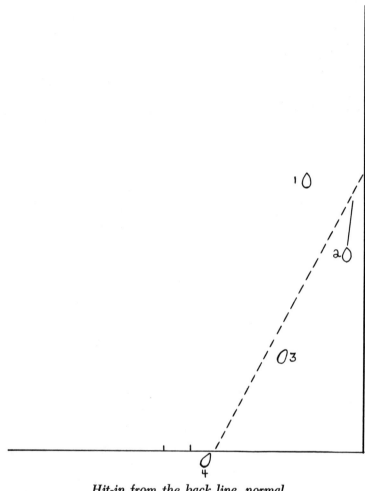

Hit-in from the back line, normal

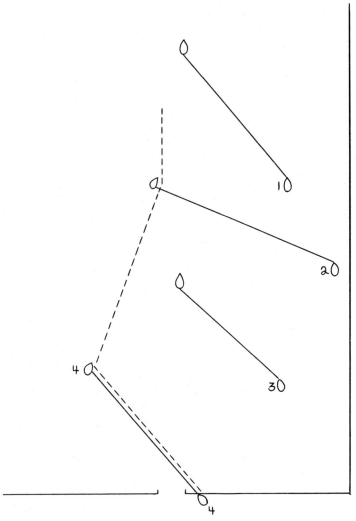

Hit-in from the back line, variation 1. Back hits to far side of field across goal posts.

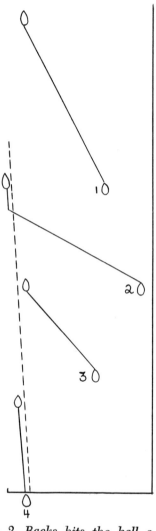

Hit-in from the back line, variation 2. Backs hits the ball a short distance, then gallops on to hit a long one which No. 2 picks up near the center of the field.

If the opponents get control of the ball on the hit-in, the situation is serious since they are within easy striking distance of the goal you are defending. In this situation each player quickly covers his opposite number and seeks an opportunity to regain the ball and resume the offensive.

This all reads a little as if it referred to football tactics and strategy. As a matter of fact, there are considerable similiarities here—passing, covering, blocking (riding off), evading, offensive and defensive areas, situations, and actions—between polo and football.

Along the Boards:

In your own defensive area, the ball is always hit toward and carried along the sideboards—but not farther than three quarters the length of the field, where it should be centered for Number One or Number Two to pick up, hopefully for a score.

There is little need for a back-up man when hitting along the boards. One or the other or both of the forwards should be forward near the center of the field to receive a pass from the boards (keeping in mind that if Number Two is hitting along the boards, Number Three should take his place), and the Back should not be drawn too far out of his defensive position near the center of the field, since this position permits him quickly to move in any direction the situation demands.

There will be occasions, however, when Number Two is on the ball along the boards, where he will be backed up by Number Three and vice versa, leaving Number One forward and the Back in the defense zone temporarily out of the play. This situation occurs when Numbers Two and Three are near each other in the vicinity of the sideboards and especially when Number Three has turned the play on the side of the field and hit (backhand or forehand) toward the boards.

Along the boards, relative positions

Offense:

At any time on the offense—when the ball is in the open anywhere from your own defensive zone to midfield—the man on the ball should have one teammate in front of him to take a pass or ride off the opposing Back, one behind him to back him up in case of a miss or of his being ridden off or hooked by an opponent, and one in a defensive position to turn the play in the event that the ball is lost to an opponent. This, of course, is easy to write or say but—in the rapidly changing situation on the field—very difficult to accomplish. To do so requires a great deal of practice and

1 O

2 O

O 3

O 4

Offense

much playing together. But perfection of this pattern assures performance well above the team's handicap.

Near the goal your team is attacking the formation is somewhat different. It is important that no one be in the way of the hitter about to score a goal, that teammates be alert to ride off or block out opponents who might interfere, and that a teammate be in position to back up the man on the ball. Who backs up and who blocks depends, of course, on who is hitting or about to hit the ball; usually this formation will involve Number One, Two, and Three but not the Back—unless he has interchanged with Number Three.

The relative positions of the players—the formation—must be flexible, since it changes frequently. The important thing is that the basic principle—a man ahead of the man on the ball to take a pass or ride off an opponent, a man behind to back him up, and a man on defence—be always observed. This is best accomplished by each player, most of the time, playing his assigned position.

Defense:

Defense is a temporary situation called for when an opponent is hitting the ball. The purpose of the defense is to take the ball away from the opponent, hit it in the direction of your goal, and put your team again on the offense.

The effectiveness of such an active defense depends on a) a "heady" Back remaining in position to take advantage of the opponents' long hits and passes, b) the other members of the team closely covering their opposite numbers, and c) all players getting quickly into the basic offense formation when the play is turned.

The greatest weakness in defense is *two* men going after *one* opponent.

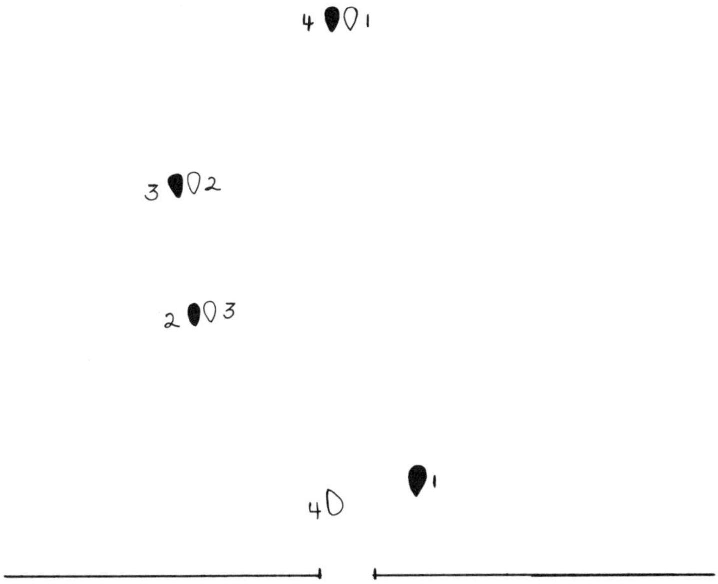

4 ◖◗ 1

3 ◖◗ 2

2 ◖◗ 3

4 ◗   ◖ 1

|_____| |_____|

Defense

SPECIAL SITUATIONS

Teammates on the Ball in Opposite Directions:

Often two teammates will be riding in opposite directions near to and almost equidistant from the ball, one with his back to the goal their team is attacking, the other facing it. Usually, the player facing the goal hits the ball. In this situation, however, it is more productive for the player with his back to the goal to back it toward the goal and the player facing it to follow the line and hit for a probable score. The advantage of this tactic is that the player facing the goal gains momentum and distance, eludes opponents, and hits the ball much nearer the goal than he would have if he had hit it at the position from which his teammate backed it.

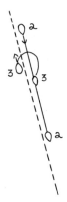

Teammates on the ball in opposite directions. Ball is traveling toward goal. White No. 2 and No. 3 are galloping on either side of the line of the ball in opposite directions. No. 3 backs the ball, telling No. 2 "Leave it and go on," No. 2 gallops on and hits a forward shot nearer the goal, No. 3 turns to back up No. 2.

Sucking in the Back:

If Number Two, approaching scoring distance, instead of hitting hard toward goal hits or dribbles the ball a short distance, he may (and usually does) cause the opposing Back to ride toward him in an attempt to take the ball from him. The Back thus leaves Number One uncovered, alone, near the goal. As the opposing Back nears him, Number Two passes to Number One who now has a clear, unobstructed chance to score. This maneuver is known as "sucking in the Back."

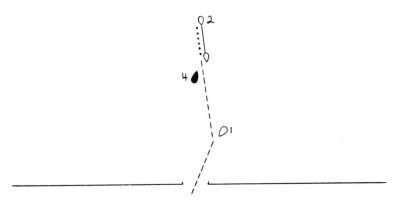

Sucking in the opposing Back

Crowded Goal:

When there is a melee in front of the goal—usually four to seven players bunched up in the 24-foot area—disengagement from the mass is desirable. This applies whether you are on the offense or the defense. If there is any semblance of team play, Number One of the defending team and the Back of the attacking team will be out of the melee. But this still leaves six players in the small goal area.

If one player moves about six feet straight out into the field opposite the middle of the goal, he can spot the ball and perhaps get at it through the crowd. Or someone may poke it out toward him (intentionally or accidentally) so that he can hit it through the goal posts or (if his team is defending) toward one of the sideboards.

After agreement is reached as to which player will normally move out of (or stay out of) a melee at goal, this "play" must be practiced until perfected.

Opponent Rides Off a Teammate:

When an opponent rides off a teammate, the backer-up

(the teammate following), stays close enough to pick up the ball if the opponent is successful, but not so close as to override the ball. (This is a common fault.)

Back Comes Through:

Occasionally, the Back will come through—galloping after the ball for successive hits instead of passing—right into the forward positions, frequently to a score. This is justified when the opponents are badly out of position and there is a clear field ahead.

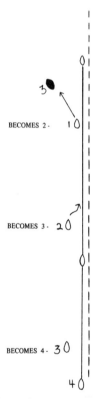

The Back comes through. No. 1 backs up the Back, No. 2 takes No. 3's normal position, No. 3 covers the Back's normal defensive position.

This situation calls for a simple shift of position backward. That is, each of the Back's teammates drops back one position: Number One becomes Two, Two becomes Three, and Three the Back. Number Two backs up the Back; Number One moves in the direction of the nearest opponent to block him or ride him off (as in football interference); Number Three takes up the Back's position and his usual defensive responsibilities.

RIDING OFF

Successful riding off of an opponent depends on a) covering your opposite number closely enough to ride him off when he might—or attempts to—interfere with your teammates' hits and b) getting *your horse's* shoulder (not yours, or your elbows) in front of *his horse's* shoulder.

Your mount needs to be bold and trained in riding off. This is covered in Chapter Seven.

You will usually ride off an opponent to clear the way for a teammate who is on the ball, or to block him from probable interference, or to clear the way for a teammate following. Occasionally, however, you will ride off an opponent to take him off the line of the ball and hit it yourself. This requires vigor and skill on your part and the part of your horse, since the opponent must be ridden well to the side to give you room to hit—frequently on your near side.

Riding off effectively can be reduced to a very simple concept: a bold horse and a skillful rider being in the right place at the right time. But one cannot come by this combination easily; it requires schooling, practice, and constant alertness on the field.

Riding off

USE OF THE DRIBBLE AND POKE

In four situations surely—and there are others—it is ineffective and usually impracticable to swing at the ball with a full stroke or even a half stroke. In these instances you need first to dribble or poke the ball a short distance. The situations are: a melee in front of goal; when an opponent attempts to hook your mallet or is in a position to do so; when you are standing still and an opponent is next to or near you; and, frequently, on a throw-in when the opposing team is lined up on your offside.

Lifting your mallet in such cases loses you control of the ball and gives it to an opponent. Poking or dribbling it gets the ball away from the mass of hooves and mallets and frees you to hit it in the open. And while it is relatively easy to hook a mallet from directly behind when you commence a full swing, it is difficult for an opponent to hook your mallet when the head is low and close to the ball.

In addition to avoiding the possibility of being hooked and in the interest of a sure hit and accuracy, it is well to dribble—and, in any event, to use a short half or quarter stroke—when you attempt to score near the goal.

DEVELOPING AND IMPROVING TEAM PLAY

It is evident that successful team play depends heavily on *passing* and on strict *position play*. Flexibility is gained through the *interchange* of assigned positions. Developing and improving effective team play requires a study and understanding of team play, sound coaching, much practice, and a lot of playing together.

First, each regular and substitute member of the team— and all aspiring members—should study and reflect on position and team play. Unhappily, the several books on the subject are all now out of print, but this chapter, it is hoped, will be helpful as a guide in this respect.

An excellent aid for the applied study of team play is a scaled diagram of a polo field, marked on a cloth or heavy paper and placed on a dining room or pingpong table. A scale of three yards to one inch would require a table about eight feet long and four-and-one-half feet wide. The players may be represented by checkers or chessmen, toy metal horses or one inch sections of an octagonal pencil. (Any of these will, of course, be larger than scale.) Four may be painted one color, the other four a contrasting color. The

A "skull session"

ball may be represented by a small hard pill or hardware nut. On this miniature field, you can set up and study a variety of situations and plays, rearranging the "players" and studying each "solution."

Next, your team needs to set up and work out situations and maneuvers, first on foot and then mounted on the field. For example, the team lines up for a bowl-in at the center of the field. The coach directs Number One to hit the ball and the other players then to take their proper positions (Number Two down field toward goal, Number Three backing up Number One, the Back to a close-in defensive position). The coach bowls the ball. Number One hits the ball only once and the other players take their positions. The coach then critiques the play, and it is practiced until it is instinctive. Then the team goes over the same routine with successively, Number Two, Number Three, and the Back hitting the ball when it is bowled in.

A similar procedure is followed for hit-ins from the back line, free hits at goal (penalty shots), carrying along the side boards, and other general and special situations.

Next, team play is applied, practiced, and perfected in scrimmages. It is important at this stage that the coach or captain (carrying a whistle) stop play when the principles of team play are seriously violated, so that the situation may be discussed and corrected.

During a match game, the coach or captain should make notes of weaknesses in the team's play, correct them in practice sessions, apply the result in scrimmages, and confirm the results in the next game.

Improving team play is just a matter of more and more and more study and practice!

12

PRACTICE: "STICK AND BALL"

Practice may not make perfect, but it is the essential base for improvement. Practice needs to be purposeful—that is, it should have immediate and long-term objectives—and it should be progressive. It should aim at strengthening what is good and correcting what is bad. It must be neither tiring nor boring.

Practice needs to be planned with respect to the desired goals, the methods of accomplishing them, time, and place.

Training aids—natural, constructed, or borrowed—will simplify and accelerate many practice sessions. Typical aids are: the "wrist strengthener" for strengthening the wrist and practicing timing when dismounted; the stationary, wooden hitting horse; a large number of used wooden balls; toy rubber balls; pylons, stakes, or standards around which to practice bending; a miniature table-top polo field like that described in Chapter Eleven.

Most important, you must budget your time to practice *regularly*.

There are three things to focus on in practice if you want to improve your game. These are: a) your mounts, b) your stroking (hitting), and c) your team play. Since much has been written on each of these subjects in preceding chapters, I'll be brief here.

During every practice session, whether your pony is well-schooled or not, it is well to practice stopping and turning, and to ride a dozen tight figures eight with flying changes. If any of your mounts shies off the ball at any stroke, or if he anticipates back strokes, spend plenty of time at a walk and slow canter correcting this. If a pony is timid riding off, schedule times for a friend to assist you in improving this condition.

Call it exercise or practice, but be sure at least twice each week to ride your mounts on long walks and trots away from a polo field, to tone their muscles and improve their temperaments and keenness.

Spend a specified portion of each practice session on the eight basic strokes (off side forward, off side back; near side forward, near side back; under-the-neck from both sides; under-the-tail from both sides). Practice your shots at a walk and at a slow canter, determining that position of the ball in relation to your pony's shoulder and hip which proves most effective in terms of distance and accuracy. Spend the greatest amount of time, of course, on the strokes which trouble you most—usually these are the near side forward stroke and the strokes under the tail. Pay attention to your timing, especially on both back shots.

It is a good idea to spend a portion of your "stick and ball" practice time on dribbling; first straight ahead on the off side, then on the near side (which is difficult) and then (very difficult) in circles on both sides. And some practice on free hits at goal from 30, 40, and 60 yards out will pay big dividends. Do this at a canter (which is what you should do in a game).

Finally, make it a practice to swing your "wrist strengthener" (see Chapter Eight) at least twenty times forward and backward on each side, every day. It takes little time and you can do this while you do other things; in thus further strengthening your wrist, forearm, and shoulder, you will improve your hitting on the field. Consider this part of your daily calisthenics. You will be aware that the strengthener is a quarter to a half a pound heavier than a mallet. This is intentional. If you are used to swinging a pound and a half, swinging only a pound seems easy.

The best—perhaps the only really effective—way to practice team play is under a good captain or coach during sessions especially devoted to it. Unhappily, such sessions are rare, and many otherwise good players are surprisingly lacking in the knowledge of the principles and in the practice of effective team play.

You can, however, learn a good deal about team play from books and by studious observation. An excellent aid for working out plays is a miniature, scaled, table-top polo field on which checkers or chessmen represent players. The plays—and your part in them—can then be tried out in scrimmages. Start with throw-ins on the center line and sideboards and hit-ins from the back lines.

Few players spend even a little time in practice. Most limit themselves to rather aimless "stick and ball" and to scrimmages. Nevertheless, practice (as outlined above) surely produces improvement. Perhaps it is worth giving it a serious go!

The only item of tack distinctly associated with polo ponies is the *boot* or *bandage* worn on the front legs as a protection against injuries from balls or mallets. Occasionally

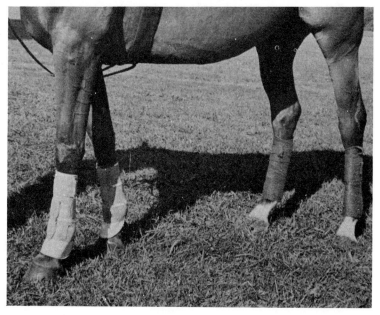

Polo pony "boots" (forelegs) and bandages (hind)

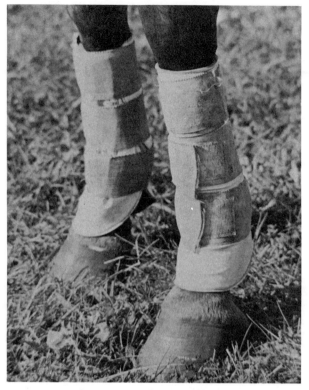

Closeup of polo pony "boots"

boots or bandages are worn also on the hind legs. Boots
for polo ponies are made of felt with elastic or leather
reinforcement, and are held in place to cover the lower
cannon bone and fetlock joint by three or four leather
or plastic adhesive straps.

Polo tack

Coolers—lightweight wool blankets—are used when the ponies are walked to cool out after being sponged and scraped at the end of the period.

Cooler

The *bridle* normally includes a caveson noseband and a pelham bit with moderate-to-long shanks, and frequently contains a port. The brow band—instead of being of plain leather as in a hunting bridle—is frequently colored and decorated with stable, club, or personal designs.

Draw Reins

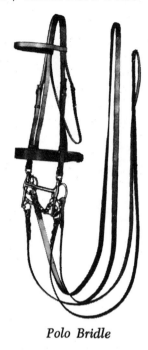

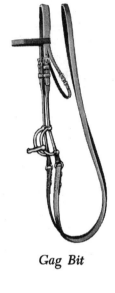

Gag Bit

Polo Bridle

Typical Polo Bits

The *saddle* is of the hunting variety with the flaps cut only moderately forward—neither so much as in the typical jumping saddle, nor as straight as in those used for saddle-bred horses. Polo saddles generally do not contain knee rolls.

The stirrup *leathers* are relatively wide (for durability and to avoid cutting into the boot or leg), and the stirrup *irons* are large and heavy.

Saddle pads are not generally used unless a horse has a sore back. They are not designed to keep the underside of the saddle clean, and it is easier to clean the underside of a saddle than a felt pad. However, if you feel that you need or want a pad, obtain one of the washable chemical fiber types and be sure to wash it after each use.

Polo Saddle

Balding Girth

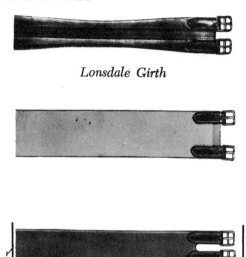

Lonsdale Girth

Folded Leather Girths

Martingales (standing martingales) are common on polo ponies. This is because of the many sudden stops and the frequent proximity of the player's nose to his mount's head and neck. A number of good horsemen on well-schooled mounts, however, play without martingales.

Some polo players use *breastplates* to insure that the saddle will not slip backward. The conformation of a number of horses makes this a wise precaution in a game requiring so much speed, such frequent changes of pace, and so many sudden stops and short turns.

There is a pernicious—or, at any rate, very dangerous—practice, indulged in by some players, which can cause serious injury. It appears to be an esoteric mark of distinction. This is wiring up the safety catches on the bars supporting the stirrup leathers. The safety catch is designed to

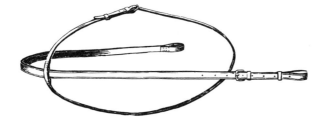

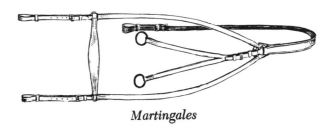

Martingales

release at about 40 pounds backward pressure. Thus, if you are thrown or fall from your horse "hung up" in the stirrup iron, the weight pulling on the stirrup leather against the safety catch will open the catch and the leather will slide off the bar supporting it.

Why then, do so many (too many) players wire the safety catches so that they will not release? The usual explanation is that they are afraid of losing a stirrup during play because of the backward swing of their legs, especially when a leg is forced backward in close contact. If the safety catch spring is kept in good order (responsive only to a full 40 pounds), the chance of losing a stirrup leather and irons while you are in the saddle is very remote indeed. I know several players who never wire up the safety catch, who have not lost a stirrup leather over a period of twenty years of regular play.

14
STABLE ROUTINE

The stabling, care, feeding, grooming, and exercising of a polo mount is generally similar to that of any light riding horse in work.

However, because of the nature of his strenuous and demanding work, special attention needs to be paid to the legs, the feet and shoes, the back, and the girth area of a polo pony. Care must be exercised to detect and treat immediately sore and swollen legs, developing corns, loose shoes, sensitive or sore backs, beginning girth galls.

The amount of grain and hay should, of course, be balanced according to each individual horse's condition and the extent of his work in practice and in games. Supplements—vitamins and trace minerals—should be added to oats or, even better, included in one of the pelleted, balanced, and enriched feeds commonly available. The protein content should be relatively high (13 to 15 percent). The usual ingredients of a balanced feed are listed here:

Crimped Oats
Cracked Corn and Corn Gluten
Barley
Wheat Middlings
Linseed Meal

Soybean Meal
Alfalfa Meal
Dried Whey
Cane Molasses
Ground Limestone
Defluorinated Phosphate
Iodized Salt
Traces of: Manganous Oxide
    Zinc Oxide
    Copper Oxide
    Cobalt Carbonate
    Iron Carbonate
    Calcium Iodate
    Calcium Pantothenate
Vitamin A Palmitate
Vitamin B12 Supplement
Vitamin E Supplement
D-Activated Animal Sterol
Choline Chloride
Riboflavin Supplement
Niacinamide
Menadione Dimethylprimidinol Bisulfite

Most pelleted feeds contain these ingredients in varying properties.

Alfalfa hay, which is rich in protein, is excellent once a horse gets used to it. Other desirable hays are mixtures of timothy and clover and of timothy, clover, and alfalfa. And no matter how nutritious, rich, balanced, and "all-purpose" a grain feed may be, a horse still needs the relaxation and calming effect of nibbling hay and of grazing. Grass, in one form or another, is a horse's only *natural* food: his entire body is designed to find and eat it—off the ground.

All horses need as much water as they will drink—on the average, about 12 to 15 gallons a day. A polo pony, because of the strenuous nature of his work, might well need more.

Except before he has been well cooled out after a game or strenuous practice session, have a full bucket of clear, cool water in his stall and, if there is not a stream running through it, a tank, large tub, or even a bucket in his paddock. Your stable routine should be planned so that your horses will drink *before* they eat, or an hour after feeding. After a game, practice, or any strenuous exercise, let your horse sip a little water from time to time as he is being cooled out, stopping at intervals as he is being walked.

Since a polo pony's profuse sweating lowers the salt content of his body (as with humans), you must be sure your pony is provided with a salt brick in his stall or feed bucket and a salt lick in his paddock.

Constantly observe each horse's condition, alertness, energy, and weight, and adjust the amount of his grain and hay when there are variations in weight and keenness. And check frequently the quality and condition of your grain and hay.

Many, perhaps most, polo players—if they are playing in match or practice games two or three times a week—turn their ponies out on the intervening days, believing they have had exercise enough. Surely this is all right. However, there is some advantage in exercising horses every day— that is, six days a week—regardless of strenuous games or practice. A *complete* letdown or rest may not be good. A slow walk of a couple of miles or a little trotting, even the day after a hard game, is both relaxing and good for maintaining muscle tone. Since polo ponies are seldom asked to trot during a game or in practice, it is good for their muscles and their disposition to trot them frequently, on small circles and figures eight and along quiet wooded lanes and dirt roads.

To prevent sores and to improve the muscle tone and general well-being of your horse, see that he is well groomed every day. You will want to use a dandy brush, a body brush, and a coarse rub rag. The time spent on this chore will pay attractive dividends to your mount—and so to you.

Most horsemen believe that a horse should be much-brushed and little-washed. Polo ponies, because of the considerable sweat they generate through strenuous exertion under a hot sun, need to be washed often and scraped before they are walked to cool out. Only two comments need be made with respect to washing: use tepid water where practical (*not* cold, in any event), and have the proper equipment immediately at hand—bucket, sponges, good scrapers. (The flexible brass straps are best.) Use different sponges, of course, for the body, muzzle, and dock. Use several good coolers (lightweight wool blankets) and keep them clean.

Tack must be kept meticulously clean, soft, and pliable, for your own sake as well as your horse's health. Broken tack—especially a stirrup, girth, or martingale—can cause critical accidents. And leather not cared for will break easily under little strain. It is good insurance to take your bridles completely apart at least once a week when you clean them, to repair promptly any part of your bridles or saddles that needs it, and to examine carefully, at least once a week, your stirrup leathers and girth straps for evidence of dryness or wear which might make them unsafe.

If someone else bridles and saddles your mount, be sure to check the adjustment of the bridle and the tightness of the girth. If your girth is loose and you reach out for an elusive ball or make a sharp turn, you might be unpleasantly surprised! If the bridle is improperly adjusted, you will get something less than his potential from your pony.

15

DRESS

The *protective polo cap* is the most distinctive item of a polo player's dress. It has a broad peak running well back on the head to provide some protection for eyes and ears as well as shade from the sun. The back of the cap comes low to the nape of the neck. This headpiece is constructed basically of heavy cork, with web straps providing an air space; the outside covering is canvas, and there is a chin strap to hold the cap in place. Polo caps are manufactured with white coverings, but many players paint them in a club color or colors—which provides easy and quick identification for a teammate—or in a personal color for individual identification.

A few players still sport the pith sun helmet, the popular headpiece formerly worn by the British Army in India. If not as colorful, the American polo cap provides more effective protection, is less bulky, lighter on the head, and less expensive.

A cotton or light wool half-sleeved *shirt* or *jersey* with a "crew" or "polo" collar covers the upper body. It is usually in solid, striped, sashed, or hooped colors, with the number of the player's position (1 to 4) on back and front.

Breeches are traditionally made of white cotton drill, chino, moleskin, or gabardine, the legs fastened with laces,

Conventional polo cap and shirt

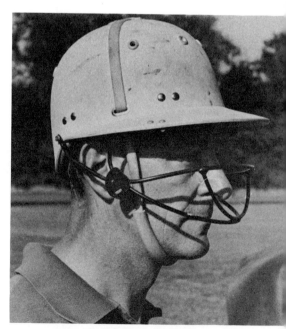

Polo cap with protective wire guard

Polo "helmet" (favored by the British)

buttons, zippers, or ribbon (tape) ties. Since laced fastenings take an irritatingly long time to tighten and adjust, and buttons loosen, fall off, and are often uncomfortable, zippers or tape ribbons (tied low down the leg) appear to be the most satisfactory fasteners.

Boots are traditionally brown and generally (also traditionally) of field boot design (with laces at the instep). Lately a high-legged western or cowboy-type boot has become popular. Some players wear conventional high brown boots.

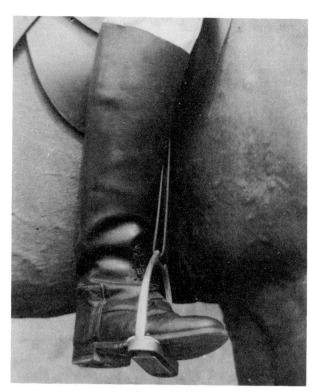

Conventional "field boot"

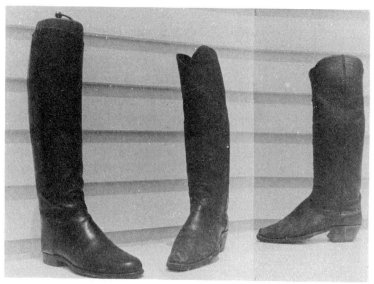

Western type polo boots compared with conventional English design

Most players wear *spurs,* since their ponies at times need considerable urging. Usually these have long shanks but no rowels. Roweled (sharp) spurs are prohibited by Field Rule Number 2 of the United States Polo Association.

Knee guards—leather padding shaped to protect the knee —are worn by many players, especially those who have sustained knee injuries.

Workmen's cotton *gloves* are worn by many players to prevent the reins and mallet from slipping out of sweaty hands.

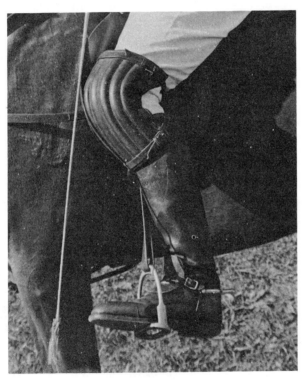

Knee guard

A very few players wear a *polo belt* for support, a piece of wool about five inches wide with leather straps and buckles to fasten it.

While it is hardly an item of dress, some players carry a *whip*—in addition to four reins—in their left hand (to supplement the spurs). The whip has a light leather thong to slip over the wrist and is about four feet long. It is made of twisted rawhide.

Informal dress is common. In "stick and ball" practice, scrimmage, and other informal practice and training sessions, all manner of gear is worn—regular (short) cowboy boots, denim "Levi's," chaps, and any old kinds of shirts. But a cap is always worn, in any kind of game.

Full regalia. On the horse, a martingale and draw-reins. The player is wearing spurs, knee guards, a glove, and a helmet, and is carrying a whip as well as the mallet. The horse's tail is "tied up" and pony boots protect his lower forelegs and bandages his lower hind legs.

16
UMPIRING

If you are asked to umpire, you will do well to accept the invitation. There are great advantages to umpiring:

1) You will gain experience in the application of the rules, the calling of fouls, and the awarding of penalties, since the immediate decision in these matters will be yours. You will find that umpiring requires following the play closely, considerable concentration, and some forethought.
2) You will have an excellent opportunity to observe the team play of two teams—usually fairly evenly-matched. You can observe what is done well and what poorly, and note specific opportunities for improvement.

You will, of course, want to prepare yourself for the opportunity by carefully and critically reading and reread-ing the rules—all of them, but particularly the Field Rules on fouls and penalties.

The following suggestions may help you as an umpire make a prompt and correct appraisal and decision.

1) Since the ends are changed after a goal is scored—that is, the goal a side (team) is attacking changes from one end of the field to the other—it is important for the umpire to keep in mind always which team

Umpire in distinctive striped shirt with ball carrier and (not visible) pick-up stick

is "going" which way. An effective and simple means of doing this is to focus on one of the ends—let's say the south. Then at all times keep in mind who is attacking the south goal. For example, "Blues are going south," or "Now Reds are going south."

2) Since crossing a player who has the right of way on the "line of the ball" is the most common foul, it is well constantly to keep in mind who has the right of way. Usually, but not always, this is the

player who last hit the ball. Being constantly aware of who has the right of way is difficult and requires a high degree of concentration, but this is the umpire's job.

3) If a player commits a foul in the third of the field near the goal his team is attacking, the penalty should be relatively light—probably a Number 5 or maybe 4 if it is unduly dangerous or damaging. On the other hand, if a player on the defending team in that same area commits a foul to prevent the opponents from scoring a goal, the penalty should be relatively severe—a Number 2 or 3 and in some instances even a Number 1. If the foul is committed between a third and a half of the field in the defensive area by a player on the defending team, it will probably rate a Number 4 penalty. So, say to yourself, for example, "Blues (the attackers in the area of the goal they are attacking) 4, 5, or 6; Reds 2, 3, or 4."

4) Keep a sharp eye out for illegal hooks and unnecessarily rough play (bumping at a dangerous angle, elbowing, etc.).

5) Do not call a foul if in your mind there is any doubt one was committed.

6) Do not hesitate to call a foul promptly when one clearly was committed—regardless of who committed it.

7) For minor infractions and in cases where no material advantage is gained or lost by either side, normally (not, of course, necessarily always) award Penalty Number 5.

Frequently the umpire is called a referee. And there is nothing seriously wrong with this. Correctly, however, the man controlling the game, mounted on the field, is an umpire. In big matches—and often in less important ones—

there are *two* mounted umpires on the field. In these cases, it is necessary to appoint a referee (dismounted and off but near the field), who will make the final decision in the event that the umpires disagree. (This seldom happens, since the umpire farthest from the play usually defers to the umpire who called the foul.)

17
ARENA POLO

Arena polo should be in your picture. Even if you started to play polo on a regulation field and even if you are still playing only on a regulation field and have never played indoors or in an "arena," it is a good idea to have some experience with the junior game. Why? Because it will present an opportunity to play more polo than is possible if your play is confined to a regulation field, and because it will sharpen your game and present an additional pleasant variation.

In beginning, as we wrote earlier, it might be well to start your career indoors or in an outdoor arena. Why? Because indoor and arena polo—compared to regulation polo—require less upkeep of facilities, less able mounts and fewer players, less speed and more handiness, and less dependence on the weather.

Arena polo, as opposed to regulation polo, may to some extent be compared with paddle tennis as opposed to regulation tennis, or perhaps to tennis on a turf court as against tennis on clay.

Again, I use the term *arena polo* here in its broadest sense to include polo played in a covered arena with four foot sideboards and a dirt footing—and polo played in a similar

Arena polo

*un*covered arena on a small field or paddock with a turf or dirt footing ("paddock polo").

In arena polo, as noted previously, there are only three players on a side and the ball—about one and a half times the diameter of the regulation wooden ball—is an inflated leather one, in appearance much like a diminutive soccer ball or basketball. In an arena, goals are scored when the ball hits a framed, solid backstop or rolls into a narrow, shallow trench beneath it. In paddock polo the inflated ball is hit through goal posts ten feet apart at either end of the field.

The arena game puts a premium on very handy ponies, quick at getting away from a standstill and after a turn, rather than those long on speed and a little short on handiness; dribbling, accuracy, "poke" shots and hits off the sideboards, and passing are very important. (Crowding in front of the goal is disastrous.)

You will improve your game, play more often, and increase your enjoyment of polo if you play both on regulation fields and in arenas.

If the grounds around your home or your stable area permit it—or if there is a fairly level field nearby which you can use—you can easily and inexpensively construct a paddock field of your own. It will provide you with a first-rate training aid, and on off days at your club's regulation field or arena you can invite a few friends over for "stick and ball" and a two- or four-period scrimmage or a "round robin."

18
MOVING UP

You need to improve four things if you want to play a better game than you now are playing, if you want to gain a handicap rating, and if you want to be asked to play in better matches and better tournaments on better teams. These four things are your mounts, your stroking, your riding off and—most important of all perhaps—your team play.

You will need faster, handier, bolder mounts than you have—and perhaps an additional mount, so that you will be playing a fresh one more often. This does not mean necessarily that you will have to acquire any new mounts. Maybe so, maybe not; it depends, of course, on the capabilities, potential, and schooling of those you have. But whatever horses you use will have to do better if you are going to move up. If your horses have the basic qualities required to become good polo ponies, then stepped-up and concentrated schooling, proper exercise, and special attention to stable management should move them up in their abilities, reliability, and stamina.

If you are thinking of buying a proven ("made") pony, keep in mind that no matter how well someone else handles and plays a pony, if you should acquire it, *you* will have to spend a lot of time schooling it yourself. A horse, like you, is an individual; you have to get to know each other. He may not do as well for you, and then again, he may do better for you than for his former owner.

Now, in order to get the most out of your improved mounts, you have to improve your stroking, the effectiveness of your riding off, and your team play.

Your stroking will improve to the greatest extent with practice—tiresome, regular, planned, repeated practice. It should involve a lot of work on the near side, a lot of dribbling, a lot of hitting on both sides of your mount at a walk and a canter. You should practice dribbling in successively smaller circles to the right on the off side and circles to the left on the near side. And you should practice some free shots at goal, at a walk and at an easy canter. The overall purpose is to increase the accuracy, length, and reliability of your hitting.

Improvement in riding off requires a companion. There are just two elements in successful riding off. They are: a) a bold, confident, unafraid horse that understands what it is doing and b) the technique of placing your horse's shoulder in front of your opponent's horse's shoulder. The development of both requires much practice, analysis, correction, and more practice. Your horse's confidence can only be developed by successful accomplishment.

Improving your team play requires much study, critical observation, keen perception, and experience in playing each position. Each time you play, recall and concentrate on the four requirements for playing your position well (see Chapter Eleven). Whenever you watch a polo match, concentrate on a position on each of the opposing teams and study critically the extent to which each of the players you are observing adheres to the principles of team play for that position. Note his effectiveness, too.

Finally, you have to do something very important and very difficult. You have to evaluate your temperament. Are you, you must ask yourself, sufficiently bold, aggressive, determined, self-confident? It is hard to alter your own or anyone else's temperament, but it *can* be improved to some extent.

In summary, moving up depends on the extent to which you are willing to—and do—study, learn, practice, and gain experience—and to the extent to which you observe and perceive critically and analytically.

19
HAVING FUN

When you have schooled a suitable horse in the elementary requirements of a satisfactory polo mount, have learned to hit the ball from both sides of your pony—forward and backward and under the neck and tail—and have learned something about teamplay, you will want to have fun playing polo. How you do this depends on the facilities available to you in your area.

If there is an established club with a full-sized, short field, or arena, in your vicinity, you should have no trouble being invited to play a couple of periods in intra-club scrimmages. If you play well and are appropriately unobtrusive, and if you have more than one mount, you will be asked to play additional chukkers and finally to play several periods, a whole low-goal match game, or participate in a low-goal tournament. While you are doing this, you have, of course, an excellent opportunity to observe, study, and learn about the game, and to profit both by things done well (which you may emulate) and things done poorly (which you may avoid).

If an established polo club or polo ground is not available, or if time, distance, or transportation provide a serious obstacle to their use and enjoyment, you might try a short paddock field of your own as described in Chapter Five.

Let us assume that you have a paddock polo field of your own. How do you use it?

First, you use your field every suitable day—early in the morning or in the late evening—for "stick and ball," to school your mount, and to improve your stroking ability and accuracy. You will want to use an "indoor" (inflated) ball.

Second, you can have a lot of fun in informal games on your field. Call them practice games, if you like. With one pony each, and three (even two) on a side, you can play three periods of six minutes each. You would rest five minutes after the first period and ten minutes after the second.

If you have enough players, you may schedule a "round robin." This employs three teams. Each plays the others for one period, so that each team plays two periods. Let us designate the teams A, B, and C. The schedule would look like this:

1st Period	A vs. B	6 minutes
Rest		5 minutes
2nd Period	B vs. C	6 minutes
Rest		5 minutes
3rd Period	A vs. C	6 minutes

The team which wins both of its matches wins the "round robin." In the event that all three win one game, the one with the largest number of goals for its two games wins. If two teams have the same total of goals scored, a "sudden death" period, limited to three minutes, is played. If the "sudden death" period does not break the tie, let it go at that and congratulate both teams on their sterling performances.

To make it easy for teammates and opponents to identify

A polo "vest"

each other, you might have a lady interested in your project make three vests of a simple color—blue, red, white, yellow, green—and another three of a contrasting color.

Where do you get the players? They will come primarily from two sources. 1) Other beginners like yourself, either in the neighborhood or at some distance and 2) Zero players —and perhaps an occasional one goaler—from a nearby club who would like to get in a little additional easy practice.

A third, and very rewarding, source is horsemen (and perhaps a few horsewomen!) whom you might interest in polo. Invite one or two to witness a scrimmage on your field or just to watch you work at "stick and ball" and tell them what fun it is and how little it costs. It should not take long to make several converts.

A polo *gymkhana* provides a lot of interest and a good deal of fun. It can be held as a separate event, in conjunction with a horse show, or preceding or following a match game or tournament. It is probably most satisfactorily staged as an independent and separate event, combined with a picnic.

Typical polo gymkhana events would include the following:

1) *Flat-Footed Start Race.* From one end to the other of a polo field.
2) *Bending Race.* From the starting line, gallop to the far end of a line of 8 poles 8 feet apart, bend through the poles toward the starting point and then back to the far end. From the far end of the line of poles gallop straight "home" past the start and finish line.
3) *Check and Turn Race.* Gallop to a marker about 60 yards from the starting line, check, turn, and gallop back and past the starting line. This contest can be conducted either in heats of four at a time plus a final or individually against a stopwatch.
4) *Walking Race.* 100 yard race in which any horse

breaking to a trot or jog, stopping, or backing is eliminated.

5) *Trotting Race.* Trot about 100 yards to a pole, then around it and back to the starting line. Any horse breaking to a walk or a canter, stopping, or backing is eliminated. This is an especially interesting contest since polo ponies seldom trot.

6) *Stationary Hitting Contest.* The contestant hitting the ball farthest from a designated line, his mount *standing still*, wins. May be conducted in a group or individually.

7) *At-A-Gallop Hitting Contest.* The contestant hitting the ball farthest from a designated line, approaching at a canter or gallop, wins. May be conducted in a group or individually.

8) *Back-Stroke Hitting Contest.* The ball—placed on a designated line—may be approached at any gait and speed and hit (backward) from either side. The contestant hitting the ball the greatest distance wins. In a group or individually.

9) *Bull's Eye.* A circle about 12 inches (18 inches if you want to make it easier) in diameter is placed about midfield. As in golf, each competitor goes in turn and the contestant placing his ball in the circle in the least number of strokes wins.

10) *Scramble.* Each contestant—limited to six at a time—is given a different colored ball. All line up at the back line at one end of the field. The winner is the contestant whose ball first crosses the back line at the opposite end of the field. Players are encouraged to hit other players' balls backward, sideward, or off the line they are traveling to prevent them from scoring.

Many horse shows, in areas where polo is played, include a polo pony class in the prize list. Entering these shows can provide interesting experience and some good fun. If you have a well-schooled horse, you need not be a good player to place in the ribbons. Usually you are requested to canter several "tight" figures eight, then gallop hard to a point, pull up, and turn promptly on the haunches. You will prob-ably—surely if you are being considered for a ribbon—be asked to ride off another entry and perhaps also to "race" him down the show ring, turn about, and race back. You will also be asked to back. Class specifications typically read like this:

Polo Ponies: Any height, weight, breed, and sex. To be judged on handiness, speed, mouth, balance, way of go-ing, manners, substance, and ability to stop in a straight line and ride off.

Polo pony class at Keswick Horse Show, Virginia

A Polo mallet must be carried and exhibitors must ride in conventional polo uniform. Tack must be that ordinarily used on polo mounts. Unusually severe bits and draw reins to be penalized.

So have fun playing polo. Whether you are engaged in a friendly scrimmage, a polo gymkhana, a polo pony class at a horse show, a match game, a round robin or a tournament—have fun. And remember that having fun is an attitude, a point of view!

20
COMPETITION

The objectives of all of your preparation and practice, naturally, are to become a member of a club team and to play with it in match games and tournaments, to be on the winning side and, one day, to earn a handicap.

Obvious. So what? Well, when you play in a match or tournament, with a lot of people—many of them your friends and admirers—watching, it's different.

In serious competition you experience a complete change from "stick and ball" and fun practice games. Now you have to "pull your weight" and do your share to achieve success for the team, because others depend on you. *You* might make or break the team effort to win. This is a considerable responsibility. You accept it, you feel it, you tighten up. You press. And here you get into trouble. You don't play as well as you can because you try too hard, because you are tense, worried, and nervous.

Your first game as a member of a team in match or tournament play will be psychologically your worst; your performance will probably suffer, too. As you gain experience in match and tournament games, the tension will diminish and your confidence will increase. But don't be concerned if you should never quite completely relax. Some old hands believe that a little tightness at the beginning of an important game is good. They like it that way.

What can you do to ease your introduction to match and tournament play, to counteract the known dangers? The following should help.

Concentrate on the game. Put to use all that you have learned so far, try to anticipate the play, turn *before* the ball is backed. Particularly when you are not near the ball, spot, keep track of, and worry your "opposite number," and be prepared to ride him off.

Don't worry. So you missed one, you were out of position when the ball was passed up to you, you failed to hook or ride off an opponent, you goofed. These things happen to everyone; there is nothing you can do about them after they happen. So forget your goofs and get on with the next play. There's much ahead, and things will get better. During rest periods between chukkers, put aside any thought or comment on what you *should* have or *might* have done.

Keep your cool. Don't get mad at your mount, at yourself, or at anyone else; not at your teammates, or your opponents, or the umpire. Getting mad accomplishes nothing useful or helpful, and, it interferes with the exercise of good judgement. Most likely, it will only generate counteraction and more misery. Take it easy.

Have as much fun as you can. After all, polo is a game. And while, of course, you want to play to win, neither the world, nor your team, nor you are going to come apart if you don't. Keep a gay spirit—make light of your troubles.

Be a gracious winner and a cheerful loser. You will find this pleasant and rewarding.

Most important in your first times in match and tournament play, don't get in over your head. Don't be so anxious to be on a team that you find yourself continually out of the play because your mount, your skill, and your experience are not up to the others on the field. This situation will be very discouraging to you and will delay further invitations to join a team.

Smilingly refuse to get sucked in over your head; start and, as you advance, stay in your class, and enjoy playing polo.

INDEX

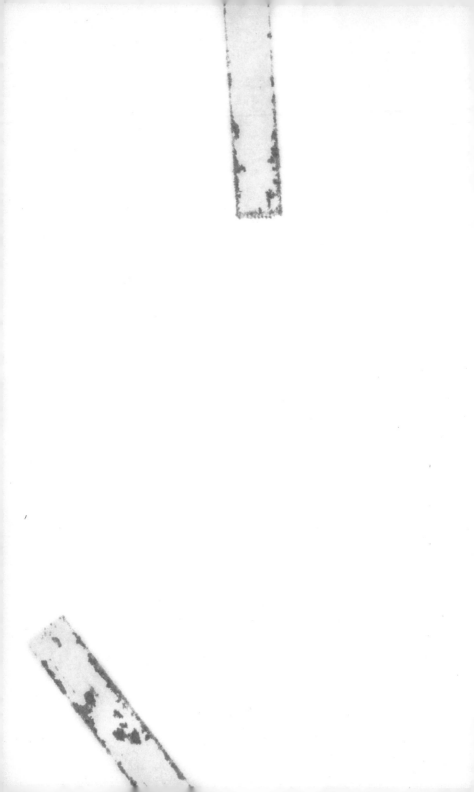